QUEEN
of common
¢ENTS

QUEEN
of common
¢ENTS

Over 1001 Tips and Facts to Save
Time and Money

MICHELLE SNOW

HEGEMONY PRESS
AN IMPRINT OF CEDAR FORT, INC.
SPRINGVILLE, UTAH

DISCLAIMER

We hope the tips in this book will be a valuable resource for you. However, Michelle Snow and Cedar Fort Publishing cannot guarantee success and disclaim any liability and damages from the use or misuse of any product, formula, recipe, or tip presented in this book. Remember to always patch test any cleaning recipe in an inconspicuous place before treating the entire surface.

ISBN 13: 978-1-59955-982-7

Published by Hegemony an imprint of Cedar Fort, Inc.
2373 W. 700 S., Springville, UT 84663
Distributed by Cedar Fort, Inc., www.cedarfort.com

LIBRARY OF CONGRESS CATALOGING-IN-PUBLICATION DATA

Snow, Michelle, 1961- author.
    Queen of common cents : over 1001 tips and facts to save time and money / Michelle Snow.
        pages cm
    Includes bibliographical references and index.
    ISBN 978-1-59955-982-7 (alk. paper)
    1. Self-reliant living. 2. Home economics. 3. Consumer education. I. Title.

    GF78.S66 2012
    640'.41--dc23

                                    2011037733

Cover design by Brian Halley
Cover design © 2012 by Lyle Mortimer
Edited and typeset by Emily S. Chambers

Printed in the United States of America

10 9 8 7 6 5 4 3 2 1

DEDICATION

This book is lovingly dedicated to the four
women who taught me in my youth how to
be a provident woman: Eunice Garbett, Ruth
Overman, Mary Swain, and Dianne Veinotte.

Coming to all major bookstores in March 2012

Summer Bucket List for Kids

Pre-order your copy today!

Other titles by Michelle include
the best-selling food storage book

*It's in the Bag: A New, Easy, Affordable,
and Doable Approach to Food Storage*

ISBN: 978-1-59955-385-6
Published by CFI, Springville, Utah

And

Gluten Free Food Storage: It's in the Bag

ISBN: 978-1-59955-489-1
Published by CFI, Springville, Utah

*The W.O.W. Diet: Words of Wisdom and
Dietary Enlightenment from Leading
World Religions and Scientific Study*

ISBN: 978-1-59955-386-3
Published by Bonneville Books, Springville, Utah

CONTENTS

Because the Garbage Man Doesn't Come until Friday

A middle-aged lady named Dianne was returning from visiting her grandchildren in California. When she exited the concourse, she saw her husband, Richard, smiling and waving by the crowded luggage carousel. After receiving a kiss, Dianne asked, "Sweetheart, anything happen while I was gone?" "Um, nothing I can think of," replied Richard as he picked up her last piece of luggage. As Dianne and Richard made their way to the parking garage, Dianne looked at Richard with a quizzical expression on her face and said, "Richard, I have been gone for a month and nothing has happened? I can't believe that!"

After placing the last piece of luggage in the trunk of the car, Richard said nonchalantly, "Oh, Adam broke his leg."

"Adam! Our son? How did that happen?"

"He tripped over the ottoman trying to get the garden hose through the back door."

Dianne's voice was anxious as she grabbed Richard's forearm and asked, "Is he all right?"

"Oh yeah. He's just fine."

Dianne let go of Richard's arm, furrowed her brow, and said, "What was he doing trying to get a garden hose into the house?"

"Oh, he needed it to put out the fire."

"THE FIRE! WHAT WAS ON FIRE?"

"The shower curtain."

With eyes bulging nearly out of her head, Dianne asked, "The shower curtain was on fire? How did the shower curtain catch on fire?"

"The east wind kicked up and blew through the window."

"WHAT?"

"You see, my dear, I opened the window to air out the bathroom and the wind blew the shower curtain into the wastebasket."

"Richard, since when do we have an incinerator for a bathroom wastebasket?"

Richard looked down and sheepishly answered, "Since I dropped a match into it."

"HAVE YOU LOST YOUR MIND?"

Richard chuckled and lovingly placed his arm around his wife's shoulders, "Sweetheart, I had to answer the phone. It was your mother."

"So, let me see if I got this right. Because my mother called, you had to drop a lighted match into the bathroom wastebasket, which caught the shower curtain on fire when the east wind blew, and this caused Adam to trip over the ottoman, breaking his leg, while trying to put out the fire with a garden hose?"

"You got it!"

Holding her head in her hands, Dianne peered between her fingers and asked, "Why did you have to throw a match in the wastebasket when my mother called?"

"Because the bathroom smelled so badly, I opened the window and lit a match to air it out," Richard nervously continued. "Just as I lit the match, the phone rang. It was your mother, so I quickly blew it out and threw it in the wastebasket."

"Do I dare ask why the bathroom smelled so badly?"

"That's easy; it smelled because I went down to the basement."

Running her hands through her hair, Dianne said, "You went down to the basement, which made the bathroom smell, which caused you to throw a lit match into the wastebasket because my mother called, which caught the shower curtain on fire when the east winds blew, which cause Adam to break his leg when he tripped over the ottoman while trying to bring the garden hose into the house to put out the fire?"

"Yes, you see, I went down to the basement to get some bottled meat for dinner. When I took the ring off the Mason jar the lid fell off in my hand, and the smell was horrible—I guess it didn't seal—so I decided to flush it down the toilet since the garbage man doesn't come until Friday!"

"So next thing you're going to tell me is that it's all *my* fault that Adam broke his leg because I bottled the meat?"

"Honey, you said it, not me!"

FREEZING

1.   Tip—Remove all possible air from foods that will be stored in a freezer. Air is one of the conditions necessary for freezer burn to develop. Here's how freezer burn occurs: The dry air removes the moisture from the food, which creates ice crystals. The loss of moisture results in dry, shriveled, and discolored food over time; the more air that comes in contact with the frozen food, the more moisture is removed and the quicker food becomes freezer burned.

2.   Fact—Freezer burned food is safe to eat. It will be drier and may taste like the freezer, but it is safe to eat. I just cut the freezer burned portion off the meat and cook the remaining meat as I normally would.

3.   Fact—Bacteria, mold, viruses, and some parasites are not killed through the process of freezing. Freezing only slows their growth.

4.   Tip—Freeze foods in small quantities so that they freeze quickly. Slowly freezing foods creates larger ice crystal formation, which breaks down the cellular structure of food and decreases the food's quality once defrosted.

5.   Tip—Never stack food to be frozen in the freezer. This delays the freezing due to the thickness of the stack. To shorten freezing times, place foods in a single layer in the freezer. Once frozen, stack as desired.

6.   Tip—Tightly wrap food that will be frozen so there is minimal exposure to air, thereby reducing the likelihood of freezer burn.

7.   Tip—When freezing liquid or semiliquid foods, be sure to leave room for expansion or the containers will split or break. I typically leave a ½ inch head space.

8.   Fact—Freezing food does not significantly decrease nutritional values.

9.   Fact—Freezers should be kept at 0°F to ensure minimal bacterial growth, rancidity, and loss of nutritional quality.

10.   Tip—Keep an appliance thermometer in the freezer to ensure a constant temperature of 0°F. Refrigerators should be kept at 40°F or below.

11. **Fact**—There are only three ways to safely thaw frozen foods: in the refrigerator, in a cold water bath, or in the microwave.

12. **Tip**—When thawing frozen foods in a cold water bath, keep the water cold and remember to change the water every thirty minutes.

13. **Tip**—If microwaving frozen foods, be sure to cook the food immediately after thawing because foods may become heated during the thawing process, which increases bacterial growth.

14. **Fact**—Frozen foods can go rancid, especially if they contain fats.

15. **Tip**—Trim excess fats from meats and then remove air by tightly wrapping meats. This will reduce the risk of foods going rancid.

16. **Fact**—According to the USDA, if food is thawed in the refrigerator, it can be safely refrozen.

17. **Tip**—Never refreeze any food that has been out of the refrigerator for more than 2 hours.

18. **Tip**—Never refreeze any food left out for more than 1 hour at temperatures of 90°F or more.

19. **Fact**—According to the USDA, it is safe to freeze leftovers within 3–4 days of cooking.

20. **Fact**—Discoloration of vegetables is caused by active enzymes.

21. **Tip**—Enzyme activity in vegetables can be halted through a brief heat treatment. This is called blanching. (See Tip #83 to learn how to blanch.)

22. **Fact**—Raw or cooked meats and casseroles can be cooked in the oven frozen. Just decrease the temperature by 25°F and increase the cooking time by 1/3 to 1/2.

23. **Tip**—Before cooking poultry, check all poultry cavities for giblet packages. Fumes from the hot packaging will flavor the bird and may be harmful to your body.

24. **Tip**—Cook giblets separately from the bird to reduce the risk of food-borne illness.

25. **Tip**—Carefully examine the underside of meat for absorbent padding before cooking.

26. **Tip**—How to cook a frozen roast: Lower the temperature by 25°F and increase roasting time by ½.

27. **Tip**—Plan on 1–1½ days per 5 pounds of meat if defrosting a turkey in the refrigerator.

28. **Tip**—If defrosting a turkey using the cold water thawing process, plan on 30 minutes per pound of meat.

29. **Tip**—Allowing 1 day per pound of meat if defrosting ground meat or chicken tenders.

30. **Tip**—A pound of meat can be thawed using the cold water thawing process in an hour or less.

31. **Tip**—A 3- to 4-pound package of meat will take about 4 hours to defrost using the cold water thawing process.

32. **Tip**—It takes only 10–15 minutes to thaw frozen shrimp using the cold water thawing process.

33. **Tip**—Keep the freezer door closed if the electricity goes out. A full freezer will typically keep its contents frozen for up to 2 days if the door remains closed. A half-full freezer typically will keep the food frozen for one day.

34. **Fact**—According to the USDA, meat that is partially frozen, has ice crystals, or has been kept at 40°F is still safe to refreeze.

35. **Tip**—Discard foods that have been contaminated with raw juices from meat, poultry, or fish.

36. **Tip**—Store your frozen meat on the lowest shelf of the freezer to prevent defrosted meat juices from contaminating other food items, should the electricity become interrupted.

37. **Tip**—When defrosting meats in the refrigerator, be sure to place them on the lowest shelf so that fruits, vegetables, and other refrigerated foods cannot become contaminated by accidental spilling of raw meat juices.

38. **Tip**—If the electricity is going to be out for long periods of time and the freezer is partially filled, cluster the frozen packages tightly together so that they will keep colder longer.

39. **Fact**—Frozen foods are safe to eat almost indefinitely; however, food quality diminishes over time.

40. Tip—According to the USDA, bacon and sausage can be frozen for 1–2 months without any loss of quality. I have kept my ground sausage for 6 months without any change in color, taste, or consistency. I have not had as good of luck with sausage links; after 4 months, they became discolored and had a slight rancid flavor. I believe this happened due to the links being exposed to air from loose packaging.

41. Tip—According to the USDA, casseroles can be frozen for 2–3 months without any loss of quality.

42. Tip—According to the USDA, eggs can be frozen for 12 months without any loss of quality. I notice a change in the eggs' consistency and flavor at 9 months: the eggs were a little rubbery and the flavor was stronger—almost fishy.

43. Tip—*Cooked* eggs become rubbery if frozen.

44. Tip—Here's how I freeze whole eggs:

Step 1: Scramble the raw egg and pour into ice cube trays.

Hint: Measure the size of your ice cube trays so you know what size egg will fit in a cube. I have one ice cube tray that holds one large egg per cube and another ice cube tray that only holds a small egg per cube. If you forget to test the size of your cubes, 3 tablespoons of thawed whole egg equals approximately one large egg.

Step 2: Once the eggs are frozen solid, pop them out of the ice cube trays and into large freezer bags.

Step 3: Remove all the air from the bag because air causes frozen eggs to become tough and rubbery.

When you are ready to use your eggs, place them in a covered bowl in the refrigerator to defrost. I usually do this the night before I need them so that they are ready for breakfast. When eggs are defrosted, they look horrible. Just re-scramble them with a fork and use them as you normally would.

45. Tip—To extend the life of your frozen eggs, invest in a vacuum sealer, or you can slip a drinking straw in the storage bag and as you close the bag, suck out as much of the air as you possibly can. Once you have removed all of the air, quickly slip the straw out as you seal the area where the straw was inserted.

46. Tip—According to the USDA, frozen dinners can be frozen for 3–4 months without any loss of quality.

47. **Tip**—According to the USDA, ham, hot dogs, and deli meats can be frozen for 1–2 months without any loss of quality. I disagree; I have found that frozen ham has a different texture and becomes watery even as soon as a week after being placed in the freezer. Therefore, I would suggest that frozen ham be used in soups and casseroles.

48. **Tip**—According to the USDA, meat can be frozen for 4–12 months without any loss of quality. Every year I purchase ½ of a beef. This meat lasts us with no change in taste, color, or consistency for a year to a year and a half. Please bear in mind that our beef lasts this length of time because the butcher wraps it with protective butcher paper, eliminates all possible air, and quick-freezes it.

49. **Tip**—According to the USDA, ground meats can be frozen for 3–4 months without any loss of quality. Again I disagree; our ground beef lasts a year to a year and a half with no change in texture, color, or flavor. You may be thinking, "But what about nutrition?" Remember that the USDA states that properly frozen foods do not have a significant loss of nutrition. So why do I get such long freezer life? Because of the methods my butcher uses to prevent air from coming in contact with my meat.

50. **Tip**—When buying meats from a grocery store, always wrap prepackaged meats with butcher paper for long-term freezer storage. Why? Because the see-through plastic wrap allows air to pass through. And remember, air is what causes freezer burn! You do not need to take the meat from its original packaging; just wrap the butcher paper over the original packaging and you will extend the freezer life of your meats.

51. **Tip**—According to the USDA, poultry can be frozen for 12 months without any loss of quality. I buy my turkeys and roasting chickens once a year, and I have never seen freezer burn.

52. **Tip**—Buy your turkeys after Christmas and you will find they cost 50 percent less money than the original price. This is true for fresh and free range turkeys too.

53. **Tip**—Don't purchase frozen packages of any fish, meat, poultry, or shellfish if the packaging has been torn.

54. **Tip**—Don't purchase frozen packages of any fish, meat, poultry, or shellfish if the packages are above the freezer line (typically 4–6 inches from the lip of the freezer).

55. **Tip**—Never buy any frozen product that has visible ice crystals; this may be indicative of poor freezing methods or foods being frozen, thawed, and then refrozen. Probably the single most common items that I find ice crystals in at grocery stores are frozen vegetables. Dig to the back of the freezer and grab a package where the vegetables aren't frozen together and doesn't have ice crystals mixed in with the vegetables.

56. **Fact**—The key to successful freezing of foods is using fresh, high-quality ingredients!

57. **Tip**—Home-baked goods can be frozen for 2–4 months. My biggest complaint is that over time, baked goods pick up the "freezer taste." Store-bought, prefrozen foods can be successfully frozen until the expiration date on the package.

58. **Tip**—You can make homemade yeast dough and freeze it for another day. So why not make a double batch and freeze one?

59. **Tip**—If I am freezing a dough that requires a double rising, I freeze it after the first rising. After it has risen the first time, I shape the dough and place it on a cookie sheet to freeze. Once frozen, I wrap the dough, label it, and then when I am crunched for time I simply take the pre-shaped loaves or rolls out of the freezer, allow them to rise for the second time, and bake as I normally would.

60. **Tip**—You can also freeze drop cookies, such as chocolate chip cookies, cinnamon rolls, and bar cookie dough. Just scoop onto a cookie sheet or slice cinnamon rolls, freeze, and place in a freezer bag until you are ready to bake and enjoy.

61. **Tip**—Most dairy products can be frozen successfully.

62. **Tip**—You can freeze overripe bananas with their skins on and use them in baked goods later. Frozen bananas are mushy after defrosting.

63. **Tip**—When milk is discounted at the store because it is near the expiration date, I snatch it up and freeze it. I use the milk for drinking, making yogurt, making cheese, and so on. I have frozen milk for 2 months with no change in flavor. Remember to thaw milk only in the refrigerator.

64. **Tip**—I buy my butter during the holidays when you can get it priced anywhere from $1.80 a pound to $2.00 a pound. It freezes well for 9 months. After that it begins to pick up the taste of the freezer.

65. **Tip**—You can freeze bricks of cheese. Only one drawback: it crumbles when sliced. This is no problem for me because I use it for quesadillas, grilled cheese sandwiches, and as a topping.

66. **Tip**—I have frozen cottage cheese for two months with no change in flavor.

67. **Tip**—Shredded cheese freezes well for about 3–4 months. After 3–4 months, it becomes dry and looks freezer burned.

68. **Tip**—I have frozen my freezer jams for up to 1½ years. The top ¼ layer sometimes is a touch drier, so I scoop it off and there is no difference in the jam below. Once again, remember that frozen food does not go bad, only the quality changes over time.

69. **Tip**—I have stored ice cream for two months with no problem. After two months I have found it begins to pick up the freezer taste and becomes a little freezer burned.

70. **Tip**—To keep opened ice cream from drying out in the freezer, tuck some wax paper on top of the exposed ice cream.

71. **Tip**—Never freeze cream, mayonnaise, or any high-fat dressing. It clumps and looks like it has curdled.

72. **Tip**—If freezing dry items, fill the containers to the very top to decrease air exposure. They will taste fresher, and it will extend the life of the frozen food.

73. **Tip**—Flour doesn't freeze, so you can use it directly from the freezer without stopping for thawing.

74. **Fact**—Did you know salt loses its savor if frozen? It does!

75. **Tip**—It's difficult to remember a month or two down the road what you have frozen, so be sure to label and date all of the containers of wonderful food you have prepared and frozen.

76. **Tip**—You can freeze soft cheeses, such as cream cheese; however, the consistency changes. I have used it in cooking, and there is no noticeable difference.

77. **Fact**—My children have never tasted store-bought baby food. I made my baby food from the foods the rest of the family was eating.

Be sure to puree the baby food before you season it to an adult's liking because spices may upset your baby's stomach.

78. Tip—You can freeze homemade baby food in ice cube trays. Pop out the pureed food once frozen and place in freezer bags. Be sure to label it or you won't be able to tell the green beans from the spinach.

79. Tip—I freeze my herbs in chicken and vegetable broth. Here's how: In a food processor, add washed herbs and just enough broth to form a paste. Place paste in ice cube trays and, once frozen, place in a labeled freezer bag.

80. Tip—I also freeze my chipotle adobo sauce, and when I need some, I use a knife and cut off a chunk. This works great because most recipes only call for a tablespoon or two.

81. Tip—You can freeze any seasoning vegetables that you are going to cook with; just mince, dice, or chop them and then freeze them on a cookie sheet. Once frozen, place vegetables in labeled freezer bags. Do not use in uncooked dishes because the cell walls of these vegetables rupture during the freezing process and look horrible once thawed.

82. Tip—Make frozen pesto with your herbs. Here's one of my favorite pesto recipes: combine 3 cups basil, ¼ cup oregano, ¼ cup rosemary, ¼ cup thyme, 2 teaspoons minced garlic, ¾ cup Parmesan cheese, and enough oil to form a paste when processed. Place in ice cube trays. Once frozen, place pesto cubes in labeled freezer bags.

83. Tip—How to blanch vegetables prior to freezing: Fill a large stockpot with 1 gallon of water per 1 pound of vegetables. Prepare another pot or large bowl with ice water. Heat water in stockpot until it comes to a rolling boil. Place washed vegetables in boiling water for the given length of time (depending on vegetable). Immediately after blanching, remove vegetables from the hot water and submerge in ice water. After vegetables have cooled, remove them from the water, pat them dry, and place them on a cookie sheet for individual pieces, or simply place them in a freezer bag and label. Remember to freeze food in single-layer packages until frozen and then stack.

84. Fact—Over-blanching causes loss of nutrition.

85. Fact—Under-blanching is worse than no blanching because vegetables will actually come out darker after freezing. Why? Because the added heat potentiates the enzymatic action.

86. **Tip**—Here's how I freeze my green beans: Wash green beans. Blanch for 3–4 minutes. Cool in ice bath. Dry. Bag green beans, removing as much air as possible with a drinking straw or a commercial vacuum sealer, and then freeze.

87. **Fact**—Did you know you can freeze corn on the cob in the freezer with the husks intact, and it will keep for 1–2 months? Yep, it's true! A corn farmer told me this and I tried it. It worked. Be sure to wrap the corn before placing in the freezer or it will pick up the freezer taste.

88. **Tip**—Here's how I freeze my cut corn: husk corn and wash. Blanch ears of corn for 4–5 minutes. Cool in ice bath. Cut off kernels of corn and bag, removing air.

89. **Tip**—Here's how I freeze my peas: remove peas from pods and wash. Blanch 2–3 minutes. Cool in ice bath. Drain and dry. Bag and remove air.

90. **Fact**—I was taught by a broccoli farmer that I didn't need to blanch my broccoli before freezing it. I tried it both ways and really couldn't tell much of a difference. If you want to compare for yourself, blanch your broccoli for 3–4 minutes, submerge it in an ice bath, and then freeze it.

91. **Fact**—I haven't had much success freezing summer squash. It turns watery when thawed.

92. **Tip**—Probably the easiest vegetable to freeze is winter squash. All you do is bake it, scoop it out of the shell, and freeze it in bags or containers.

93. **Fact**—The only fruits I have frozen are peaches, rhubarb (which is technically a veggie), apricots, and cherries. All I did was wash the fruit and add some lemon juice (about ¼ cup per gallon bag) and enough sugar to coat the fruit. Juice will form as you are filling the bags. Before placing in the freezer I just mixed the juices around.

94. **Fact**—Some fruits require chemicals to halt enzymes from darkening frozen fruit.

95. **Tip**—Vitamin C found in lemon juice or other commercial products containing ascorbic acid can be added to halt the discoloration caused by naturally occurring enzymes in the fruit. I have even tried vitamin C tablets, but it didn't work very well.

96. **Tip**—Gelatin dishes weep—liquid droplets ooze—if frozen.

97. **Tip**—Fried foods don't remain crispy if frozen.

98. **Tip**—Frostings made with eggs become sticky if frozen.

99. **Tip**—Meringue becomes tough if frozen.

100. **Tip**—Leafy vegetables such as spinach and beet greens can be frozen. Just cook them, cool in an ice bath, and package.

101. **Tip**—Nuts can be frozen in shell or out. Remove air and they can last for 2–3 months.

102. **Tip**—Nuts with hard to crack shells, such as Brazil nuts, will crack more easily if cracked while frozen.

103. **Fact**—Roasted nuts have a shorter freezer life than raw nuts.

104. **Tip**—Cabbage can be chopped and frozen in bags if you are going to use it in soups.

105. **Tip**—Custard-based foods become watery and lumpy if frozen.

106. **Tip**—You don't have to thaw frozen vegetables before cooking them.

107. **Tip**—Clean your freezer regularly according to the manufacturer's instructions. While cleaning it, place frozen foods in coolers, discarding damaged or severely outdated items.

108. **Fact**—Most people do not know the temperature of their freezers. Be safe; an appliance thermometer is inexpensive and ensures that your frozen food is being stored at correct temperatures.

109. **Tip**—Want a pitcher of lemonade that doesn't dilute over time due to ice melt? Fill ice cube trays with lemonade and freeze. When ready to serve, fill pitcher with lemonade and lemonade cubes, and no ice cubes are needed.

110. **Tip**—Here's my recipe for lemon-lime-ade: juice of 2 large lemons and 3 good-sized limes, 5½ cups water, ⅔ cup crystalline fructose, **but do not use high fructose syrup (HFS)**. Crystalline fructose is not the same thing as HFS! If you do not have crystalline fructose, you may substitute white sugar but increase to 1 cup.

111. Tip—Brown sugar stored in the freezer doesn't clump over time.

112. Tip—Do not use artificial vanilla to sweeten foods that will be frozen. The flavor changes.

113. Tip—Sage becomes bitter if frozen.

114. Tip—Garlic and onions should not be frozen raw; their flavor changes.

115. Tip—Cloves become stronger in taste if they are frozen.

116. Tip—My father worked as a baker and a cool trick he taught me was to freeze my round cakes before frosting. They are much easier to handle and less likely to crumble while frosting.

117. Tip—You can speed up the defrosting time of frozen dough to about an hour by placing in a warm oven (170°F).

118. Tip—Quiche freezes well for 1–2 months.

119. Tip—For a fun punch, freeze fruit slices and cherries in ice cubes or a gelatin mold filled with punch.

120. Tip—Crepes can be frozen for up to 4 months. Separate crepes with parchment or wax paper and store in a freezer bag, removing as much air as possible. The tender edges of crepes break easily, so protect them by placing in a container. Do not separate crepes until completely thawed.

121. Tip—You can thaw crepes in the microwave.

122. Tip—Do not freeze filled crepes; they become soggy.

123. Tip—If you have a frozen fish fillet that has been forgotten in the back of the freezer, make fish stew or fish cakes (use same as you would crab in crab cakes but substitute fish fillet for crab). Remember, frozen food doesn't go bad; just the quality of the meat decreases (that is, changes color or becomes drier).

124. Tip—To whip cream more effectively, beat whipping cream in a tall bowl that has been chilled in the freezer along with the beaters.

125. Fact—Heavy cream doesn't freeze well.

126. Tip—Heavy cream that has been whipped and dolloped onto wax paper freezes well. Just allow 10–15 minutes to defrost. Or for a fun treat, place a frozen whipped cream dollop on top of a steaming mug of hot chocolate.

127. Tip—To keep whipped cream from separating on cream pies in the summer, fold in a packet of unflavored gelatin.

128. Tip—For an outdoor dinner on a hot summer's day, place salad plates in the freezer until ready to use. The cold salad plates keep green salads from wilting during the meal.

129. Tip—To reduce freezer odor, place an opened box of baking soda on a shelf.

130. Tip—Change the freezer's odor-eliminating baking soda every 3 months.

131. Tip—During the summer, keep tumblers in the freezer to make your summer drinks even more cool and refreshing.

132. Tip—Some seeds, such as hollyhocks and many wildflowers, require freezing conditions before they will germinate; to create this environment, place seeds in a plastic bag and store them in your freezer until spring.

133. Tip—Harvesting your garden seeds is easy and inexpensive, and it provides you with a sustainable source of vegetables; however, you must pasteurize beans and peas for 48 hours in the freezer to kill any eggs that pests have laid.

134. Tip—To quickly skim fats from soups, stews, and gravies, place them in the freezer. In no time the fat will be solidified and you can easily scoop it off.

135. Tip—Homemade fruit leather, if protected from air, lasts up to 1 year in the freezer.

136. Tip—Freeze your stainless steel and steel wool pads in a bag, and they won't rust.

137. Tip—Vinegar ice cubes will reduce sink odor and clean the blades of the garbage disposal. Freeze vinegar in ice cube trays. Place vinegar ice cubes in garbage disposal, and turn on disposal while running water.

HOME CANNING

138. Tip—When my European friends ask for my favorite recipes in metric measurements, it takes some time to convert them from US customary measurements. This little chart speeds things up. *(For example, to convert 3 tablespoons of vinegar to metric, multiply 3 by 15 to get 45 ml.)*

To change	To	Multiply by
Ounces (oz.)	Grams (g)	28
Pounds (lbs.)	Kilograms (kg)	0.45
Teaspoons (tsp.)	Milliliters (ml)	5
Tablespoons (Tbsp.)	Milliliters (ml)	15
Fluid Ounces (fl. oz.)	Milliliters (ml)	30
Cups (C.)	Liters (L)	0.24
Pints (pt.)	Liters (L)	0.47
Quarts (qt.)	Liters (L)	0.95
Gallons (gal.)	Liters (L)	3.8
Fahrenheit (°F)	Celsius (°C)	Subtract 32 then divide by ⅝.

139. Fact—Bacteria, mold, yeast, and enzymes are the major causes of food spoilage.

140. Tip—According to the USDA, low-acid home-canned foods should be boiled for 10 minutes before consuming.

141. Tip—Carefully inspect canning bottles before using. Discard any with nicks or cracks.

142. Tip—Remember to wash your bottles with hot soapy water and thoroughly rinse before filling.

143. Tip—Bottles need to be heated for 10–15 minutes prior to filling to decrease breakage. I run mine through the dishwasher and remove them one at a time as I fill them.

144. Tip—Never boil canning lids; only simmer. Boiling damages the rubber, which will result in bottles not sealing properly.

145. Fact—*Cold Pack*: the food item and liquid or syrup is cold when placed in the canning bottle.

146. Fact—*Hot Pack*: The food item and liquid, syrup, or broth is heated to boiling prior to being placed in the canning bottle.

147. Fact—*Head Space* is the amount of space below the top rim of the canning bottle.

148. Fact—Did you know that a bottle is conveniently marked at ¼-inch, ½-inch, and 1-inch marks? The first ridge from the bottle lip is the ¼-inch mark. The next ridge is the ½-inch mark and lastly, where the neck meets the top portion of the bottle is the 1-inch mark.

149. Fact—An agricultural extension is a federally operated agricultural network that provides scientific, educational, and consumer resources at little or no charge. As a consumer, you will have access to expert knowledge such as gardening, food preservation, finance, and emergency preparedness.

150. Tip—To find the nearest agricultural extension in your state, visit http://www.csrees.usda.gov/Extension/ and remember the old adage, an ounce of prevention is worth a pound of cure.

151. Tip—Basic Instructions for Canning

1. Examine canning bottles for nicks or cracks and discard if found.

2. Wash bottles in hot soapy water or in dishwasher.

3. Place canning lids in a pan of simmering water. Keep water scalding hot until ready to use, but do not boil.

4. Prepare food according to recipe.

5. Pack food into bottle leaving a ½ inch of head space for most

vegetables. Leave 1 inch of head space for corn, peas, lima beans, meats, poultry, and fish. Fruits should have a ½ to 1½ inch of head space, depending on type of fruit being canned.

6. Add liquid.

For fruits: add boiling syrup over fruit, leaving a ½ to 1½ inch of head space, depending on type of fruit being canned.

For vegetables: add boiling water and salt, leaving a ½ inch of head space.

For meat, poultry, and fish: add 3 or 4 tablespoons liquid or broth. When raw processing, do not add liquid. For both raw and precooked meat, poultry, and fish, leave 1 inch of head space.

7. Using a clean cloth, wipe rim of bottle clean of syrup, seeds, juice, broth, and so on.

8. Place canning lids on top of filled bottles. The rubberized ring goes next to the bottle lip.

9. Place screw band on top of lid and bottle. Firmly tighten by hand.

10. Process according to recipe, altitude, and time table instructions included with your pressure canner or water bath canner.

11. Remove bottles from canner and place 2–3 inches apart on a cooling rack, or several layers of towels, to cool. Do not set bottles in cool drafts or on a cold or wet surface, as bottles may break.

12. When bottles have cooled for 24 hours, remove screw bands. Test to make sure they have properly sealed by pressing on the center of the lid. If the center of the lid does not move when depressed, the bottle is sealed. If there is any movement, the bottle did not seal and contents should be refrigerated and eaten within a short period of time.

13. Mark on top of lid with a permanent marker the date that the food was processed and what the food is (for example, *Pears 1/2010*).

152. Tip—Boiling Water Bath Time Chart–increase processing time if the time called for is:

Altitude	Less than 20 minutes, add:	20 minutes or more, add:
1,000 feet	1 minute	2 minutes
2,000 feet	2 minutes	4 minutes
3,000 feet	3 minutes	6 minutes
4,000 feet	4 minutes	8 minutes
5,000 feet	5 minutes	10 minutes
6,000 feet	6 minutes	12 minutes
7,000 feet	7 minutes	14 minutes
8,000 feet	8 minutes	16 minutes
9,000 feet	9 minutes	18 minutes
10,000 feet	10 minutes	20 minutes

153. Tip—To effectively process foods in a boiling water bath, foods must be processed for a specific number of minutes under boiling water that is at least 2 inches above the bottle lid.

154. Fact—Boiling water bath recipes state processing times based on a sea level altitude. (See tip 152 for processing time additions above sea level.)

155. Fact—A boiling water bath is recommended for processing fruits, tomatoes, and all high-acid foods.

156. Tip—Many tomatoes on the market these days have low-acidity levels. Low-acid tomatoes need to have the acidity increased prior to canning. This may be done by adding vinegar or lemon juice. I was taught by my grandmother to add 1 tablespoon lemon juice per pint and 2 tablespoons of lemon juice per quart of tomatoes.

157. Tip—Begin timing boiling water bath processing when the water begins to boil around the jars.

158. Fact—Botulism is caused by a bacterium named *Clostridium botulinum*.

159. Fact—Not all food-borne illnesses from home-canned food is caused by botulism.

160. Fact—According to the Centers for Disease Control and Prevention, an average of 145 cases of botulism are reported each year in the Unites States, with 15 percent of the cases being caused by foods that were incorrectly processed by home canners.

161. Fact—Botulism can be treated; however, severe cases have resulted in death. The signs and symptoms for botulism may include double or blurred vision, drooping eyelids, slurred speech, difficulty swallowing, dry mouth, and muscle weakness. If you should experience any of these symptoms, be sure to tell the emergency room physician that you are a home canner and, if possible, provide the hospital with the bottle and any leftover food that was eaten. Through testing the bottle and food, the hospital can determine if *Clostridium botulinum* bacteria were in it.

162. Tip—For more information on botulism, please visit, http://www.cdc.gov/nczved/dfbmd/disease_listing/botulism_gi.html

163. Fact—A sealed lid does not protect you against botulism.

164. Fact—The number of minutes that food must be pressure processed is determined by the altitude where the food will be processed.

165. Tip—Pressure Canner Altitude Chart:

Altitude:	Dial Gauge:	Weighted Gauge:
0–1,000 feet	11 pounds	10 pounds
1,000–2,000 feet	11 pounds	15 pounds
2,000–3,000 feet	12 pounds	15 pounds
3,000–4,000 feet	12 pounds	15 pounds
4,000–5,000 feet	13 pounds	15 pounds
5,000–6,000 feet	13 pounds	15 pounds
6,000–7,000 feet	14 pounds	15 pounds
7,000–8,000 feet	14 pounds	15 pounds
8,000–9,000 feet	15 pounds	15 pounds

Source: *BALL: Blue Book of Preserving*

166. Fact—A pressure canner must be used to process vegetables, meats, and all low-acid foods.

167. Fact—To ensure proper temperature and pressure within a pressure canner, you must vent for 10 minutes before processing.

168. Tip—Buy a bottle lifter; it will save your fingers from burning, and they only cost around $6.95.

169. Tip—If the glass of a bottle has a discoloration, soak it in a solution of 1 cup vinegar to 1 gallon of water. If the discoloration remains, the bottle is more than likely etched.

170. Tip—When investing in a canning funnel, be sure to spend a few dollars more for a stainless steel model. Stainless steel doesn't scratch, stain, or crack; therefore it is more durable than plastic canning funnels.

171. Fact—Bacteria cling to rough surfaces more easily than smooth stainless steel; therefore, stainless steel canning funnels are more hygienic than plastic ones.

172. Tip—Never reuse canning lids. You are increasing the risk for false seals, and why risk wasting your product, time, and health to save a few pennies?

173. Fact—To effectively process foods in a pressure canner, use a time and pressure table to determine the number of minutes that food needs to be processed at a specific number of pounds of pressure.

174. Fact—Times and pressures are determined by the altitude where the food item will be pressure cooked. If your friend lives in California and pressure cooks something for 10 minutes at 10 pounds of pressure, and you live in Colorado, you will discover that the time and pressure tables will have you pressure cook the same item at a higher poundage.

175. Fact—Pressure gauges should be tested yearly for accuracy.

176. Tip—Many emergency preparedness stores, specialty kitchen stores, and extension services will check pressure canner gauges for free.

177. Tip—Vegetables for canning: Select fresh, firm vegetables. Do not bottle overripe vegetables because they will have a soft texture and will be at a greater risk for spoilage.

178. Fact—Vegetables **must** be processed in a pressure canner. It is important that you carefully read the recipe and process accordingly because the risk of botulism increases with vegetables not correctly acidified or processed.

179. Fact—If your corn turns brown after processing, you processed it at too high of a temperature and caramelized the sugar in the kernels.

180. Tip—When using a pressure canner, thoroughly read the included instructions for operation and determine how long and how many pounds of pressure should be used at your elevation.

181. Tip—The head space for most vegetables is a ½ inch; however, corn, peas, and lima beans require a 1-inch head space.

182. Tip—Fruits for canning: select fresh, firm fruits. Do not bottle overripe or bruised fruits as they will have a soft texture and will be at a greater risk for spoilage.

183. Fact—Fruits should be processed in a boiling water bath. Fruits may be cold packed or hot packed.

184. Tip—The head space for fruits is ½ to 1½ inches depending on fruit, so read the recipe carefully.

185. Tip—Fruit that doesn't seal immediately after processing can be pureed and made into pancake syrup or ice cream topping.

186. Tip—My trick for not having the Maraschino cherries bleed out in my fruit cocktail is to leave the stems on and layer the bottle pears, pineapple, peaches, Maraschino cherries, peaches, and so on. Layering the Maraschino cherries between the peaches protects the pears should bleeding occur.

187. Recipe—Maraschino Cherries

10 cups pitted Royal Anne cherries, reserving juice

2 tsp. alum

4 Tbsp. salt

8 cups cold water

7 cups sugar

2 oz. red or green food coloring

1 tsp. almond extract

Wash and drain cherries. Pit and drain but save juice. Dissolve alum and salt in 8 cups cold water. Add cherries. Let stand for 6 hours. If cherries float, weight them down with a plate so that they are submerged. Drain and rinse cherries. Measure juice and add water to make 2 cups. Add sugar. Heat until it has dissolved. Add cherries. Boil 2 minutes. Remove from heat. Add food coloring and extract. Let stand for 1 day in a cool place. Heat to boiling and then ladle into prepared jars. Process 5 minutes at sea level (refer to water bath canning chart for the correct processing time for your altitude).

188. Tip—Meats, poultry, and fish for canning: meat, poultry, and fish should never be coated in flour or bread crumbs before bottled; this increases the risk of food poisoning.

189. Fact—Meat, poultry, and fish must be processed in a pressure canner.

190. Fact—You may raw pack or hot pack meat according to the recipe.

191. Tip—Raw-packed meats, poultry, or fish should not have any liquid added to the bottle prior to processing.

192. Fact—You can bottle meat with bones, like chicken and fish.

193. Tip—If the meat, poultry, or fish has been cooked prior to bottling, you may add 3–4 tablespoons of water, juice, or broth.

194. Tip—The head space for meat, poultry, or fish is 1 inch.

195. Fact—Flat sour is a condition that occurs when food is allowed to sit too long before it is processed. Flat soured foods will seal properly.

196. Fact—Some contaminated foods will appear spoiled only once heated. If home-canned foods *ever* look or smell not quite right, *DO NOT TASTE THEM!*

197. Tip—If you are a history buff, you may enjoy this website which outlines the early history of USDA canning recommendations: http://www.uga.edu/nchfp/publications/usda/review/earlyhis.htm

198. Tip—If you need inexpensive canning bottles, here are some places to look: garage sales, estate sales, thrift shops, flea markets, classified ads, farmers markets, and the best way is by word of mouth. I have been given many bottles by people whose grandmothers have passed on. Be sure to tell them not to empty the full bottles. That's your job! They benefit by less work, and you benefit by having canning bottles. It's a win-win situation!

199. Fact—Nicolas Appert first invented canning food in 1810.

200. Fact—John Landis Mason invented the Mason bottle.

201. Tip—Antique canning bottles have a surprising market value. Here is a website that will assist you in determining your bottle's value: http://www.sha.org/bottle/food.htm#Canning/Fruit%20Bottles.

202. Tip—David Hinson has done a remarkable job explaining canning jars in his article, "A Primer on Fruit Bottles." Here's the website: http://www.av.qnet.com/~glassman/info/b&e/primer.htm.

203. Fact—It takes three ingredients to make jelly: pectin, acid, and sugar.

204. Tip—If you don't have a juicer or steam juicer, do it the old fashioned way: wash the fruit, crush berries or grapes, and heat. Once piping hot, place in a damp jelly bag, doubled cheesecloth, or muslin and allow juice to drip into a bowl.

205. Fact—Lemons, grapefruit, sour plums, blackberries, and sour grapes all have enough pectin and acid naturally so that you can make jelly just by adding sugar and boiling the combination until it sheets off of a cold spoon.

206. Fact—Boil jelly over a fast, hot heat. Slowly boiling destroys the pectin.

207. Fact—Sure-Jell and MCP are manufactured by Kraft General Foods.

208. Fact—Many home canners are fiercely loyal to a particular brand of pectin. In our house, it is MCP or nothing! You might be surprised to learn that the ingredients are different.

209. Fact—Freezer jams and jellies made with low-sugar or no-sugar pectin don't freeze as well as full sugar pectin recipes.

210. Fact—No-sugar or low-sugar pectin recipes have a shorter shelf life than regular sugar recipes.

211. Tip—Never use low-sugar or no-sugar pectin when making low-acid jams or jellies such as jalapeño, zucchini, or pumpkin because it will increase the risk of botulism and other food-borne illnesses.

212. Tip—Low-sugar or no-sugar pectin recipes can be sweetened with apple juice concentrate, artificial sweeteners, white sugar, or fructose.

213. Tip—For any MCP or Sure-Jell pectin questions call 1-800-437-3284.

214. Tip—Ball Canning (Jarden Home brands) home canner's hot line: 1-800-240-3340.

215. Tip—Helpful jam, jelly, and preserving websites: www.kraftfoods.com, www.freshpreserving.com, www.mrswages.com.

216. Tip—Pectin jams and jellies typically do not set if the batch is doubled.

217. Tip—Never decrease the amount of sugar in a jam or jelly recipe using pectin. If less sugar is desired, purchase no-sugar or low-sugar pectin.

218. Tip—To ensure a firm set, use ½-pint or pint bottles. Jams and jellies bottled in quart bottles tend to have a looser set due to the jelly taking longer to cool.

219. Fact—Liquid pectin is made from apples.

220. Fact—Underripe apples have more pectin in them than ripe or overripe apples.

221. Fact—Our great-grandparents didn't have the luxury of running to the store for pectin. They simply made their own.

222. Tip—Here's how to make your own pectin: Take underripened apples or crabapples and slice into quarters. Fill a cooking pot almost to the top with the apples. Cook over moderate heat, stirring every 20 minutes or so. When apples are cooked and look like applesauce, pour into a colander covered with a flour sack dish towel or cheesecloth and place over a collection bowl. Allow to drip overnight. The clear slimy stuff that drips out is pectin. Do not squeeze the flour sack to get more pectin out.

223. Tip—To tell if the homemade apple pectin is the correct concentration, drop some of the cooled pectin into a little rubbing alcohol. If it stays gelled, then it's perfect. If it is a loose blob, it will make a loosely set jelly. If it is runny, return it to the pot for more cooking until it is reduced by about ½ the volume.

224. Tip—If you don't have any alcohol, mix 2 teaspoons sugar and 1 tablespoon Epsom salts with 2 tablespoons of your cooked pectin. Stir and allow to rest 20 minutes. If the pectin gels, it is ready.

225. Tip—Once you know your pectin is the right concentration, add fruit juice and boil until it gels. You can tell that it is right by dipping a spoon into the mixture, and if the mixture sheets off or hangs on a cold spoon, it's just right.

226. Tip—Typically the ratio of homemade pectin to fruit juice is ⅔–1 cup of pectin to 4 cups of juice.

227. Tip—If using a low-acid fruit, be sure to add 2 tablespoons of lemon juice to 2 cups of fruit or fruit juice.

228. Tip—Homemade pectin can be refrigerated for use the next day or can be frozen.

229. Tip—When making jams and jellies with homemade apple pectin, you want the ratio to be 4 cups of fruit juice plus ⅔–1 cup apple pectin to 7 cups of sugar. Boil, and it is ready when it rises up the pot rapidly and has a layer of foam.

230. Tip—You can add ½ teaspoon butter per batch of jelly to decrease foaming.

231. Fact—A bushel of apples = 48 pounds. Once canned, it will give you 16–20 quarts.

232. Fact—A bushel of cherries = 56 pounds. Once canned, it will give you 22–32 quarts.

233. Fact—A bushel of peaches = 48 pounds. Once canned, it will give you 18–24 quarts.

234. Fact—A bushel of pears = 50 pounds. Once canned, it will give you 20–25 quarts.

235. Fact—A bushel of plums = 56 pounds. Once canned, it will give you 24–30 quarts.

236. Fact—A bushel of tomatoes = 53 pounds. Once canned, it will give you 15–20 quarts.

237. Fact—A bushel of green beans = 30 pounds. Once canned, it will give you 15–20 quarts.

238. Fact—A bushel of topped beets = 52 pounds. Once canned, it will give you 17–20 quarts.

239. Fact—A bushel of topped carrots = 50 pounds. Once canned, it will give you 16–20 quarts.

240. Fact—A bushel of peas = 30 pounds. Once canned, it will give you 12–15 quarts.

241. Fact—If the top peaches of a process jar turn dark, they were not processed long enough or at a high enough temperature to halt enzymatic action.

242. Tip—I recycle my canning lids and rings by using them to cover my homemade yogurt as it ripens.

243. Tip—Canning lids that have been used for freezer jam are still fine to use for boiling bath or pressure canning.

244. Tip—To remove canning lids that are firmly stuck together in the package, simply soak them in hot water for a few minutes.

245. Fact—I had someone give me a case of lids to use that was 30 years old. Unfortunately only 50 percent of my bottles sealed, which resulted in a lot of pancake syrup being made. Moral of the fact: lids do age and eventually deteriorate, even if they look fine.

246. Fact—Canning bottles are made of tempered glass. This means they can withstand both extreme heat and cold temperatures.

247. Fact—Vegetables need to be packed loosely in jars because heat penetration is difficult to achieve.

248. Fact—You don't need to add salt to vegetables or meat before processing.

249. Tip—If your pears are discoloring after canning, next time you can add 1 tablespoon lemon juice to each quart.

250. Fact—Floating fruit is caused by using overripe fruit, processing too long, using too high of heat, using too much sugar in syrup, or packing fruit too loosely into bottles.

251. Fact—Soft pickles may be caused by failing to remove end blossom, not completely submerging cucumbers beneath the brine solution, using too weak of vinegar or brine, or precooking cucumbers at too high of a temperature.

252. Fact—Shriveled pickles may be caused from salt solution being too strong, too much sugar, or too strong of a vinegar solution.

253. Tip—When making pickles, do not use iodized salt or your pickles will have dark spots. Use pickling or canning salt.

254. Tip—If you happen to have a steamer juicer that doesn't come with a steaming chart, here is one to help you out:

Fruit	Steaming time in minutes
Apples	80
Apricots	60
Blackberries	50
Cherries	60
Chokecherries	90
Crabapples	90
Cranberries	70
Grapes	60
Peaches	60
Pears	70
Plums	60
Raspberries	60
Rhubarb	60
Strawberries	50
Tomatoes	60

PRESSURE CANNERS

255. Tip—There are many types of pressure cookers. If you are wanting to home bottle, it must be of the canner variety.

256. Tip—You can pressure cook foods in your canner; however, you may not home bottle in a pressure cooker that isn't a canner.

257. Fact—Pressure canners require varying amounts of water for processing. Read the instruction booklet to find out, or if you have lost your booklet, call the manufacturer.

258. Tip—Never pressure can on a flat-top stove. The weight may crack it, and your stove warranty will be void.

259. Tip—Never use an oven as your heat source for a pressure cooker or canner.

260. Tip—Do not use any outdoor gas burner or gas stovetop over 12,000 BTUs.

261. Tip—To keep your pressure cooker from getting a buildup of minerals, add 2 tablespoons of vinegar to the water.

262. Tip—If the inside of your pressure cooker is tarnished, you can usually get it looking better by mixing 1 tablespoon cream of tartar to one quart water, filling it no more than ⅔ full. Place lid on and heat to 15 pounds of pressure. Remove from heat and allow to set for 3 hours. Using a stainless steel scrubbing pad that is infused with soap, scrub thoroughly, rinse, and dry.

263. Tip—If the outside of your pressure canner isn't as shiny as it once was, just polish it up with some silver polish, found in most grocery stores.

264. Tip—Before canning, make sure the vent pipe is clear. Do this by placing it up to your eye; it will appear as though you are looking through a straw. If it is clogged, run a pipe cleaner gently through it.

265. Tip—These foods should never be pressure cooked because they may block the vent pipe, overpressure plug, and cover lock (note: not all models have cover locks or overpressure plugs): applesauce, cereals, pasta, split peas, barley, cranberries, and rhubarb.

266. Tip—If you are cooking foods in your pressure cooker, never fill above ⅔ full. If you are cooking foods that expand, such as rice, never fill more than ½ full.

267. Tip—Remember to open your pressure canner lid away from your body so that you are not burned by the residual steam.

268. Tip—Never force a pressure canner lid open. The result will be a long stay at the local hospital's burn unit, or worse.

269. Tip—To help protect your pressure cooker's gasket while not in use, store the lid upside down. If you choose to not place the lid upside down, remove the gasket during storage.

270. Tip—If your pressure canner is not building pressure, check to see if you forgot to put the gasket in the lid.

271. **Tip**—If you are having difficulty sliding the pressure cooker gasket into place, try lubricating it with a drop or two of vegetable oil.

272. **Tip**—Do not use vegetable oil every time you insert the gasket into the lid or it will swell and stretch out of shape.

273. **Tip**—If pressure doesn't build, and you have the gasket in place, it may have shrunk.

274. **Tip**—Here's when you need to purchase a new gasket: steam escapes from the lip of the lid and pressure is not building up, the gasket is no longer soft, or the gasket has stretched out of shape and no longer fits the lid.

275. **Tip**—To maintain the life expectancy of your gasket, remove it from the lid and wash it after canning.

276. **Tip**—Gaskets and overpressure plugs should be replaced every three years.

277. **Tip**—Never reuse a blown overpressure plug!

278. **Tip**—Overpressure plugs can shrink over time. If it becomes shrunken, dry, or brittle, replace it.

279. **Tip**—Inexpensive places to purchase pressure cookers are garage sales, thrift stores, and flea markets. If many people home-can where you live (therefore limited the supply available in second-hand sources), consider checking the aforementioned stores while on vacation.

280. **Tip**—Whenever I buy a used canner, I change out the gasket, sealing ring, and overpressure plug before using.

281. **Tip**—Remember to place the bottle rack on the bottom of the canner or your bottles will break during processing.

282. **Tip**—Never place hot bottles in cold, wet, drafty areas or they may break. I place my bottles on layers of terry towels to cool.

283. **Fact**—Pouring water into a hot, boiled-dry pressure canner may crack it.

284. **Fact**—If you are experiencing a loss of liquid from your bottles, it may have been caused by pressure reduced too rapidly, lids not properly tightened, too high of a temperature, too high of pressure, or overfilling of the bottle.

285. Fact—Loss of liquid does not impact the food's quality as long as the bottle is properly sealed.

286. Fact—Canning rings should be finger tightened only.

287. Fact—If your bottles are breaking during processing, it may be a result of overpacking, cracks in bottles, bottles touching the bottom or sides of the canner, lids overtightened, or using grocery store food bottles (such as mayonnaise bottles).

288. Tip—For better soups, pressure can the meat, stock, and vegetables in separate bottles. When ready for your soup, just open the bottles into a cooking pot, reheat, and serve.

289. Fact—Mold can only form if it has oxygen; therefore, if you have a bottle of food that is growing mold, it did not seal properly and is spoiled.

290. Fact—Sometimes you will find black stuff on the underside of the lid after opening a bottle of processed food. Don't worry: the food is still safe to eat as long as you have a properly sealed bottle.

291. Fact—Some meats form more gelatin than others; if you find some of your bottled meat congealed and others not it is because of varying amounts of gelatin.

292. Tip—Between batches, allow the canner to cool or it may be difficult to get the lid back on for the next batch of processing. This is because even metal expands when heated.

293. Fact—The Hermetic Fruit Bottle Company was founded in 1903 by Alexander H. Kerr.

294. Fact—The Kerr Company was sold to the Ball Company in 1992 for $70,000,000.

295. Fact—Jarden Home Brands owns both Ball and Kerr canning bottles. Ball Home Canning website: http://www.freshpreserving.com.

296. Tip—National Center for Home Food Preservation: http://www.uga.edu/nchfp/publications/publications_usda.html.

DEHYDRATING FOODS

297. Tip—When looking for a food dehydrator, make sure that it has an enclosed heating element.

298. Tip—To meet all dehydrating and drying needs, purchase a dehydrator with a temperature control setting that has a range from at least 90°F to 160°F.

299. Tip—Be certain that your dehydrator has a fan.

300. Tip—Make sure that drying racks are removable.

301. Fact—My dehydrators don't have timers. Many times I have to set my alarm clock so that I can turn off my dehydrator in the middle of the night.

302. Tip—If you can find a dehydrator with a timer and it is reasonably priced, BUY IT!

303. Fact—Aspartame loses its sweetness when dried.

304. Tip—If you don't have a dehydrator, you can still make fruit leather sheets by doing it in the oven. Here's how: Take 2 cups of fruit puree, add honey to desired sweetness, add 2 tablespoons lemon juice, and mix until combined. Pour on a cookie sheet lined with plastic wrap. Place in a warm oven until the center of the fruit leather no longer indents when gently pressed with your finger. Remove from cookie sheet while warm, roll up, and store in an airtight container.

305. Tip—What is a *warm* oven temperature? Here's a guide that teaches you what *warm*, *slow*, *moderate*, *hot*, and *very hot* ovens are (Now you can cook those old-fashioned recipes your great-grandma passed down to you!):

Warm oven	130°F–170°F
Slow oven	300°F–325°F
Moderate oven	350°F–390°F
Hot oven	425°F–475°F
Very hot oven	475°F–550°F

306. Tip—For a variation, add nuts, coconut, chocolate chips, or flavorings to your fruit leather before drying.

307. Tip—For a heartier snack, spread cream cheese or peanut butter onto dried fruit leather and roll up.

308. Fact—I pretreat fruits with lemon juice before dehydrating.

309. Tip—If pretreating fruits with lemon juice before dehydrating, the ratio of the solution should be equal parts of water to lemon juice. Allow the sliced fruit to soak for 10 minutes before dehydrating.

310. Tip—Pineapple does not require pretreatment. Just peel, slice, and dehydrate. Wear gloves if you are slicing several pineapples because the acid is hard on hands.

311. Tip—Only dehydrate fully ripe fruit that has no bruising or mold.

312. Tip—Homemade raisins are wonderful; however, you must boil the grapes before you dehydrate them. Be sure to boil them only until the skins break open slightly. The grape skins generally break open within a minute or less of submerging.

313. Tip—Other fruits that need to be submerged in boiling water before dehydrating are plums and cherries. I have never dried figs, but I have been told that they need to be submerged in boiling water also.

314. Tip—Never test warm fruit from the dehydrator for doneness. Only test for doneness once dried fruit has cooled to room temperature.

315. Tip—Fruit is sufficiently dried when it is leathery but not hard or crispy.

316. Tip—If you are sun-drying your fruit or vegetables, pasteurize them in the freezer for 48 hours to kill any insects or deposited eggs that may have contaminated your foods while they were drying.

317. Fact—To successfully sun-dry foods, the weather must be without rain and be at least 98°F.

318. Fact—While living in Arizona, I once burned my fruit black as coal while sun-drying on a dark-shingled roof in the middle of summer.

319. Tip—When using your oven as a dehydrator, have the temperature as close to 150°F as possible. Prop the door open a few inches and place a fan pointed into the opening to aid air circulation.

320. Fact—Dehydrated fruits when rehydrated will return to their original volume.

321. Tip—When rehydrating dried fruits or vegetables to use in a recipe, any water that is not absorbed can be used as part of the recipe's fluids. This gives extra flavor to the recipe.

322. Fact—I dry my fruit at 130°F. I haven't had much success with sun or oven drying, so I finally broke down and bought a moderately priced dehydrator, and life is good!

323. Fact—Dehydrating fruits and vegetables does not change the calorie content.

324. Fact—Dehydrating fruits and vegetables does not change the fiber content.

325. Tip—A beneficial food-dehydrating website is the National Center for Home Food Preservation: How do I dry? http://www.uga.edu /nchfp/how/dry.html.

326. Tip—Only select vegetables in their prime for dehydrating.

327. Tip—Vegetables need to be dehydrated until they are brittle and hard as rock.

328. Tip—Some vegetables do not require blanching, such as garlic, mushrooms, onions, and peppers.

329. Tip—Herbs can be placed on a plate to dry, or the sprigs of herbs can be hung upside-down in a paper bag that has paper punch holes through it.

330. Tip—To make dried herbs burst with flavor, break them up before adding them to the pan.

331. Tip—I read that you should blanch tomatoes before dehydrating. I don't, and they have not turned dark and have dried beautifully each year.

332. Tip—Celery needs to be blanched for only 2 minutes.

333. Tip—Here are some vegetables that require a 3–4 minute blanching before dehydrating: green beans, corn, and peas.

334. Tip—Broccoli (quartered and sliced) and carrots (sliced and peeled) should be blanched for 4–5 minutes before dehydrating;

potatoes (diced) should be blanched for 6 minutes.

335. Tip—Remember to wash, cut, and blanch your vegetables before dehydrating.

336. Tip—Grocery store butchers will slice your meat in any thickness you desire free of charge. I just select my meat and ask them to cut it to the thickness of jerky. This saves me a lot of time.

337. Tip—Jerky is finished drying when it cracks but doesn't break in two.

338. Tip—Jerky can be frozen in airtight containers for up to one year. If possible, vacuum-seal all foods that go into your freezer.

339. Tip—We make our jerky using round or sirloin steak with very good results. Either will do, I just buy whichever one is less expensive.

---

340. Recipe—Beef Jerky by Trent Snow

I come from a family where the men make deer jerky every fall. I happened to marry a man who makes a delicious beef jerky whenever the children ask him to. Here is my husband's jerky recipe:

2 lbs. lean beef

½ cup soy sauce

½ cup Worcestershire sauce

1 tsp. liquid smoke

1 Tbsp. red wine vinegar

1 tsp. garlic powder (not salt)

1½ tsp. onion powder (not salt)

1¼ tsp. ground black pepper * (not powder)

⅛ tsp. cayenne pepper *

Trim meat completely of fat and cut across grain into slices ⅛ inch thick (I let the butcher do this). Blend all ingredients except meat in a bowl. Dip each piece of meat into marinade, coating well. (If you have time, you may want to soak your meat in the sauce overnight in the refrigerator.) Dehydrator method: Arrange meat on trays in single layer and Dehydrate 10 to 12 hours, depending on thickness. Store jerky in plastic bags or in tightly covered containers in cool, dry area. Oven method: Place the meat strips on drying racks. Do not overlap the strips to ensure good air circulation. Leave the oven door cracked open about

---

one inch to keep the air dry. Oven temperature should be set around 150°F for the first few hours. After that it may be lowered to 130°F until dry. Place aluminum foil or a baking sheet underneath the drying rack to catch the drippings. When cool, it should crack when bent but not break. Makes about 35 pieces.

* If you like your jerky spicier, use ¼ tsp. cayenne pepper and 2 tsp. black pepper.

ODIE THE OUTBACK
OSPREY SAVES THE BAY

There was an inlet on the south side of Australia called Bountiful Bay. Bountiful Bay was a wonderful place to live, especially if you were a seagull. In fact, there was everything a seagull would want. There was a sandy beach for basking in the sun. There were pebbles of all sizes and colors to make nests. There were springs bubbling with fresh cool water. And best of all, there were schools and schools of fish in the bay. The first explorers that discovered the bay named it Bountiful Bay because it had more resources than any other bay in the world. Bountiful Bay was home to many animals; however, this story is specifically about the 391 seagulls that lived there.

Our story begins on Tuesday. Tuesday began like any other glorious morning; a gentle breeze was blowing, the sun was shining, and the father seagulls were swooping down into the crystal blue waters gathering up fish for their families. Fishing all day is difficult work, but the father seagulls didn't seem to mind because every evening after returning home from the ocean, they knew they would be hugged by their chicks and kissed by their wife for their dedication.

While the father seagulls were out fishing for the family's food, mother seagulls would busily tidy up their nests. After the nests were clean, the mother seagulls focused their attention on teaching their chicks to fly. For in this seagull colony, every father knew his role, and that was to provide fish for his family; and every mother knew her role, and that was to prepare her chicks for the day they would leave the nest.

Sally and Sam Seagull were no different than other seagull parents. They dreamed of each chick growing up, learning to fly, and providing for themselves. They even secretly looked forward to the day when they would become grandparents. Unfortunately, as fate would have it, Sally and Sam were given a most unusual challenge. That challenge was a chick named Sebastian. Sebastian was not like the other chicks living in their parents' nests—Sebastian was thirty years old. Sebastian had been taught to fly by his mother, and in fact, Sebastian was a very skilled flyer. Flying was not the problem; the problem was that Sebastian simply refused to leave the nest.

Sebastian spent his days with his large beak wide open accepting food from his hardworking father. Sebastian lounged around on the sand while his mother tidied up the nest. And when Sebastian's mother asked for help gathering pebbles for next year's nest, Sebastian would often reply, "Oh, I will be right there." But in fact, Sebastian somehow never flew over to help his mother until she had gathered the last pebble. Sam and Sally were not alone in dealing with their challenging situation. In fact, many of the other seagulls in the Bountiful Bay colony had the same problem with their grown chicks; they simply refused to leave their parents' nests.

This particular Tuesday morning, as Sam circled above his nest, he smiled down at his chicks as they opened their sweet little beaks in anticipation of breakfast. When Sebastian saw his father descending, he opened his beak too. After feeding all of the younger chicks, Sam turned to his oldest chick, and while looking into his large, gaping beak tersely said, "Son, no fish for you today! Sebastian, it's time that you move on with your life. It's time you become independent and start taking care of yourself. It's time you start catching your own fish. My heavens son, you're thirty! Have you no respect?"

Sebastian slowly closed his huge, gaping beak, turned his head, and, looking at his mother, sobbed, "Mother, do you feel this way too?" Sebastian continued as a single tear slowly formed in his eye and rolled down his feathered cheek, "Well, Mother—do you?"

"Ssson," began Sebastian's mother, "You are thirty years old, and most chicks your age have already moved out of the nest." At hearing this, Sam stomped his webbed foot and angrily howled,

"My gosh Sally, stop coddling the boy! 'Most chicks?' He's not a *chick*, he's a grown gull!" At hearing his father's abrasive yet truthful words, Sebastian did as he always did when his parents brought up the topic of moving out of the nest. He screamed and beat his chest with his wings and stomped over to his side of the nest until his mother came over to apologize for the truth his father had said.

"Sebastian, it's okay. You can stay a little longer—until you get your wings under you. Your father loves you very much. He just doesn't understand that the world has changed since he was a young gull. Would a nice shrimp make you feel better?" Sebastian put on his sweetest puppy dog face and, with his lower beak trembling, answered, "Yes, Mommy, a shrimp would make me feel better." And as it always was, just as his mother would start to fly off in search of a shrimp, Sebastian would yell to her, "Make it two!"

Sally flew high into the sky and thought to herself, *What am I going to do? Sam is right. Sebastian should be out of the nest and on his own.* Sally's thoughts were interrupted when Sam appeared by her side.

"Honey, I am sorry for losing my temper today, but it's time I take Sebastian by the wing and boot him out of the nest; he'll never leave if I don't."

"Sam, he's our chick. Maybe it's my fault. Maybe he has psychological damage from when that gale caught him and blew him off course. Maybe it's because he almost drowned that day we were floating in the bay." Sam glared and bellowed, "Or maybe he's taking after your brother! You know Sully didn't leave the nest for years, and he never helped your parents around the nest either!" Sally started to cry.

"You leave my brother out of this Sam."

"I'm sorry Sally; I am just frustrated and tired of being used by our own son! He just thinks that by virtue of his existence, he is entitled to everything. It's got to stop!"

After a few minutes of thought, Sally placed her wing tip in the air and said, "I have an idea! Let's help him build a nest not far from ours. You could even take him fishing—one on one."

"Okay, but I think a good swift kick in the tail feathers would be a better option!" said Sam with a wink. Soon, Sally and Sam were back at the nest with the two shrimp that Sebastian had ordered.

After Sebastian had eaten his two shrimp and Sam was in a better frame of mind, Sam said, "Sebastian, how about we go fishing together? You know, a little father and son time?"

"Not right now, Dad, those shrimp haven't settled so well on my stomach. I think a nap over there under the palm tree with my friends is what I need."

Sam narrowed his eyes as he barked, "Sebastian, you need to learn to fish for yourself. Your mother and I shouldn't wait on you wing and foot!"

"Yes you should!" Sebastion yelled back. "I didn't ask to be hatched into the world. So it is your responsibility to take care of me!" and off Sebastian stormed toward the palm tree.

Sally began, "Sam, did you have to . . . ," but she couldn't finish her sentence because Sam had flown off in a huff. Sally tried to take her mind off of the situation by busying herself with mindless household tasks.

Meanwhile, under the palm tree, Sebastian and his friends were all complaining about how rough it was at home, when Gid made a suggestion.

"Hey, why don't we use reverse psychology? Why don't we try to 'fish'? We can fly around, taking in the sights, and after a while return to the nest and tell our parents that fishing was bad."

"Not a bad idea. It would give us a little peace and quiet, and our parents couldn't complain that we weren't trying to pull our weight," mused Sebastian. "I like it. I like the way you think, Gid." Gid folded his wings behind his head and smiled a big cheesy smile as he basked in the admiration of his friends. Not long after, Sebastian hopped up, brushed the sand from off his feathers and flew to his parents' nest.

Dramatically, Sebastian perched in front of his parents, and after clearing his throat announced, "I have been thinking about what you said, Dad, and I think you are right. I should help out more around here, and I can start by fishing for the family. In fact, I am going to start right now!" And off Sebastian flew. Sally looked at Sam, and Sam looked at Sally, and both gulls began flapping and squawking for joy at their son's newfound independence!

Once in the sky, Sebastian was joined by his friends Gid and Sabrina, "What should we do now?" questioned Gid. "I bet our parents are watching us. Let's fly around and every now and then pretend to dive down into the water after a fish." After keeping this charade up for over an hour and spending more time pretending to fish than it would have taken to actually fish, Sebastian and his friends became bored, hungry, and tired.

"Have you ever noticed that island before?" asked Sabrina as she pointed toward a large gray fishing boat anchored in the mouth of the bay.

"No, but let's go investigate. It might be a great place to hide while our fathers are fishing," smirked Gid. Inquisitively, the three friends circled above the fishing boat.

"What a strange island. What do you think those creatures are doing with those nets?" Little did Sebastian, Gid, or Sabrina know, but those nets were going to change their lives forever.

"I'm going down for a closer look," said Sebastian as he dived down and landed on the massive rigging. Sabrina and Gid were not going to miss out on all of the fun, and soon they were perched beside Sebastian watching the men pull in nets full of plump, juicy fish.

"Would you look at all of those fish!" said Sebastian in amazement.

"That much fish would feed the colony for a year!" exclaimed Sabrina.

Gid in his excitement swooped off of the rigging, snatched a fish from the net, and gobbled it down in mid-flight.

"Hey, what are you waiting for? They're delicious!" Quicker than a blink, Sabrina and Gid were filling their bellies with fish too. As the day turned to dusk, Sebastian reminded his friends that they needed to bring some fish back to the colony. As the threesome readied to fly back to Bountiful Bay, Sabrina cooed, "We will certainly get a hero's welcome when we bring all of these fish back!" Perhaps for a kind heart or out of the need of entertainment, the ship crew welcomed their hungry feathered beggars and gladly shared their catch.

All through the night, Sebastian, Gid, and Sabrina pranced and flapped their wings as they told fishing stories. Sebastian puffed out his chest feathers and strutted on the beach as his father bragged that his son had caught the largest catch of fish in the history of Bountiful Bay. Tired and full from their adventures, Sebastian, Gid, and Sabrina fell fast asleep.

In the morning, Sebastian and his friends set out for the boat to show their fathers, Sam, Kip, and Tom. Once above the ship, Sam said to the others, "This is not an island. I don't know what it is, but it is not an island." Sam continued, "Tom, what do you think? Is it safe?"

"I don't know. I have never seen anything like it before."

Kip squawked at Sabrina not to go down to the ship, but it was too late. Sabrina, followed by the others, had landed on the ship's deck and was busily filling her stomach. After watching for a few minutes, Kip and Tom joined in. Sam hung back, eying the crew. After ten minutes Sam helped himself to a fish, and as he perched on the rigging, he thought to himself, *There is no free lunch. What's the catch?*

That evening as the colony gathered for dinner, Sam rose and said, "I am concerned about those creatures sharing their fish with us. There has got to be a price. There is always a price. There is never a free lunch! They may act like they are our big brother, but they are not. I suggest we continue living as we always have, fathers catching fish for their families." At hearing Sam's speech, the colony began to laugh. And some jeered, "Sam, if it's between you and 'Big Brother' I'm siding with Big Brother!" Sally gently tugged on Sam's tail feathers as she told him, "Let it go and have some fish, dear." Sam sighed and sat down, but he refused to eat.

A short while later, Tom came over to where Sam was brooding and said, "Sam, you have been a friend to me for many years. Take some advice and stop worrying. Enjoy the moment. We can always go back to our old ways if 'Big Brother' turns his back on us." Sam looked at his old friend and quietly said, "Maybe you are right."

Month after month, Sebastian, along with all of the other adult seagulls from the colony, would fly to the fishing boat and return to Bountiful Bay with food from 'Big Brother.' One day after returning with Big Brother's handouts, Sam looked down at his beloved colony and realized that society had changed. Fathers were no longer fishing or teaching chicks how to fish for themselves; instead, fathers were doing what they wanted to do and not what needed to be done for their families. Home life had drastically changed because mothers were no longer tidying up or gathering pebbles for next year's nests; they were too busy flying to Big Brother's to bring back fish because they couldn't depend on their husbands to do it.

Fathers and mothers were not the only ones changing. Even the chicks were changing; they seemed less respectful toward each other and toward parents and elders. Sam thought about this and wondered if it might be because no one was at the nest to care, teach, and discipline the chicks. Life at Bountiful Bay had changed, and this made Sam cry.

One night in the middle of winter, a fierce hurricane blew across Bountiful Bay. Most of the seagull colony was lost. All that remained were five unhatched eggs, Sabrina, and Sebastian. Hungry and heartbroken, Sabrina turned to Sebastian and said, "Sebastian, I need to stay here with these eggs we found. Please go to Big Brother and bring us back some fish." Off Sebastian flew to where Big Brother had been anchored, but Big Brother was not there. Sebastian flew as far as he could fly but could not find Big Brother. Finally as the sun was beginning to set, he returned to Bountiful Bay, hungry and discouraged.

When Sebastian landed near Sabrina, immediately she knew something was dreadfully wrong.

"Sebastian, what's wrong?" Sebastian, stunned at the fact that Big

Brother was no longer there, quietly whispered, "He's gone. Big Brother is gone and so is our food. Sabrina, I don't know what we are going to do."

Sabrina choked back her tears and, trying her hardest to be brave, answered, "You will fish for our food, just like my father did and your father did before Big Brother came."

"Sabrina, I never learned how to fish. My father tried to teach me, but I would always make up some stupid excuse as to why I couldn't go with him. Sabrina, my father was right. He told me there was no free lunch; that there is always a price, and you know what? That price was our ability to take care of ourselves. Sabrina, we are going to starve." It was a very cold and hungry night for Sebastian and Sabrina.

In the morning, Sebastian woke with a start when something kicked his leg and exclaimed, "Hi ya, mate!" Sebastian rubbed his eyes and saw standing before him an osprey.

"What are you doing here?" he asked.

"The hurricane blew me off course, and I crash landed here. Where am I?"

"You are at Bountiful Bay. Now who are you?"

"Crikey, I couldn't have had better luck! Bountiful Bay! I have heard about Bountiful Bay and its wonderful fishing. Oh, pardon my manners. Name's Odie. Odie, the outback osprey."

Sebastian extended his wing and mournfully continued, "Odie, I hate to burst your bubble, but Big Brother is gone, and so are all of the fish." Odie put his wing above his brow as he scanned the bay, "Mate, I think you might be suffering from heat stroke; can't you see all of those fish in the water just waiting to be caught?"

Sebastian walked away from his visitor too humiliated to admit that he had never learned to fish. Sabrina motioned to Odie to come over to where she was dutifully tending to the five surviving eggs.

"Mr. Odie, Sebastian never learned how to fish. Instead we depended on Big Brother to fish for us. Now Big Brother is gone and we are starving."

Odie the outback osprey straightened his posture and stuck out his feathered chest as he proudly announced, "Ma'am, you will never starve as long as I am alive. Now where did that husband of yours go?" And off he marched in search of Sebastian.

Finally Odie found Sebastian perched under the shade of a palm tree holding his head in his wings.

"May I ask what are you doing here when there is a beautiful soon-to-be mother gull to feed? Let's go fishing!" Sebastian felt that there was no reason for putting on airs since he would more than likely be dead in a day or two from starvation, so he confessed that he never took the time to learn how to fish. Odie the outback osprey was a kind old bird and reassured his humiliated friend that if he could teach seven clutches of ospreys how to fish, he could certainly teach one seagull how to fish. At hearing this, Sebastian laughed with renewed hope and hopped to his feet.

As they began to soar into the sky, Sebastian looked down at Sabrina, dutifully sitting on the surviving eggs, and deep inside his heart, he knew he could do it. Sebastian knew he could learn to fish for Sabrina and the chicks because that's what seagulls do at Bountiful Bay—they provide for their families.

SOMETHING'S FISHY
ABOUT THESE SAVINGS

Fish and seafood can be added to your food storage if you know when to buy them and how to freeze them. You may be wondering why a provident living book has recipes featuring expensive fish and seafood. The answer is twofold: First, a good food storage system not only has canned foods (which last for years) and protein substitutes such as a variety of grains, legumes, and beans (if stored off the cement in airtight containers, they last for decades), but also should include a selection of fresh foods, meat, vegetables, and fruits. Yes, you read correctly, *fresh foods!* And secondly, expensive items such as fish and seafood can be inexpensive if you know when to buy them and how to freeze them. Properly freezing fresh foods not only provides variety and healthful nutrition for your family but can also reduce your food budget by nearly 50 percent! In my freezer, you will find a wide variety of fish, meat, seafood, and poultry.

341. Fact—According to the US Food and Drug Administration (FDA), fish and shellfish are part of a healthy diet.

342. Tip—Fresh fish and shellfish should not smell like ammonia.

343. Tip—Fresh fish and shellfish should have a mild smell. (Before I buy, I always ask the clerk to allow me to smell my purchase before it is wrapped. If I buy something prewrapped, I smell the package.)

344. Tip—Fresh fish and shellfish should be firm and bounce back when gently pressed with your finger.

345. Tip—Fresh fish scales should be bright and shiny.

346. Tip—Eyes of fish should be clear and full, not sunken in and cloudy.

347. Tip—Fresh fish gills should be bright red, never dull or maroon in color.

348. Tip—Juices from fresh fish and shellfish should never be milky; if they are, the fish is old.

349. Tip—Fresh fillets should be moist, never dry.

350. Recipe—Almond Crusted Trout

1 (6-oz.) pkg. Reese onion and garlic croutons,
    processed into crumbs

1 (5-oz.) pkg. diced almonds

2 Tbsp. fresh thyme, chopped

2 Tbsp. fresh rosemary

1 tsp. dill

1 tsp. tarragon

3–4 lbs. trout fillets

1 cube butter, softened

wedges of lemon

Preheat oven to 450°F. Mix all dry ingredients together. Wash and pat dry trout fillets. Brush on butter. Press crumb mixture into both sides of the fillet. Place on a parchment-lined cookie sheet. Bake for 10–15 minutes, or until center of fillet is flaky. Remove from oven and spritz with fresh lemon wedge.

351. Tip—Fresh fish fillets are not discolored with yellow, gray, or green.

352. Fact—According to the FDA, "if the catch has been left out in the sun too long—or the fish haven't been transported under proper refrigeration—toxins known as scombrotoxin, or histamine, can develop. Eating spoiled fish that have high levels of these toxins can cause illness."

353. Fact—According to the FDA, most seafood should be cooked to an internal temperature of 145°F.

354. Tip—To tell if fish is adequately cooked, cut the fish at the thickest part, and if the flesh is opaque and flaky, it is done.

355. Recipe—Shrimp Salad Sandwich

½ lb. salad shrimp

⅓ orange or yellow bell pepper

1 stalk chopped celery

½ tomato, chopped

2 Tbsp. chopped fresh cilantro

2 Tbsp. chopped green onion

2 Tbsp. mayonnaise

½ tsp. Old Bay Seasoning

dill rye bread, toasted

Mix all ingredients and spoon onto toasted dill rye bread.

356. Tip—To tell if shrimp and lobster are cooked, cut open in the thickest part, and if flesh is pearly white, it is cooked.

357. Tip—How to de-vein and butterfly shrimp: hold the shrimp in your nondominant hand. Run a sharp knife down the arched back to just above the tail. Do not cut completely through the flesh to the under belly of the shrimp. You will now see near the top of the back a black line running from where the head was cut off to the tail. This is the vein. Gently scrape out the vein with the tip of your knife. Rinse and prepare per recipe directions.

358. Recipe—Coconut Shrimp with Garlic Chili Dip

1 lb. large shrimp, deveined, shelled, and steamed

3 eggs, whisked in a small bowl

Crumbs:

1 cup Panko bread crumbs

¾ cup shredded coconut

Flour mixture:

⅓ cup white flour

½ tsp. salt

½ tsp. pepper

1 tsp. paprika

oil for frying

Dip:

½ cup apricot-pineapple jam

1–2 Tbsp. Thai sweet chili sauce

2 Tbsp. water

Butterfly shrimp, leaving tail attached. Mix crumbs ingredients in a small bowl. Mix flour mixture ingredients in a separate bowl. Dredge shrimp in flour mixture. Dip in whisked egg. Place in crumb mixture and gently press crumbs into shrimp. Deep fry at 350°F until crumbs are golden brown, 1–2 minutes. Remove and place on paper towels. Serve with dipping sauce.

359. Recipe—Easy Shrimp Bisque

1 tsp. minced garlic

1 stalk celery, sliced

½ medium onion, chopped

⅔ cup mushrooms, sliced

2 Tbsp. oil

2 cups milk

1 pt. heavy cream or half and half

1 Tbsp. lime juice

1 tsp. Old Bay Seasoning

3 chicken bouillon cubes

½ lb. salad shrimp

½ cup diced fresh tomatoes

¼ cup cilantro

Thickener:

2 Tbsp. corn starch

½ cup cold water

In a pot, cook garlic, celery, onions, and mushrooms in oil until tender. Add remaining ingredients and heat to desired temperature. If desired, thicken.

360. Recipe—Cheesy Garlic Biscuits

2½ cups white flour

2 Tbsp. baking powder

1 Tbsp. dried parsley

2 tsp. sugar

½ tsp. garlic powder

5 Tbsp. oil

¼ tsp. salt

⅔ cup plain yogurt

⅔ cup water

1 cup sharp cheddar cheese, grated

Garlic butter:

¼ cube butter

½ tsp. garlic powder

Topping:

½ cup Parmesan cheese

1 Tbsp. dried parsley

Biscuit Directions: Preheat oven to 400°F. In a large bowl, add dry ingredients and mix. Add wet ingredients and cheese. Drop by heaping tablespoons onto parchment-lined cookie sheet. Bake for 12 minutes.

Garlic Butter Directions: Melt butter and add garlic powder. Brush on hot biscuits. Sprinkle generously with Parmesan cheese topping.

361. Tip—To tell if sea scallops are cooked, cut the center of the scallop, and if flesh is white and firm, it is cooked.

362. Recipe—Simple and Delicious Sea Scallops

1 lb. sea scallops, rinsed and patted dry

4 Tbsp. butter

½ Tbsp. minced garlic

salt and pepper

wedges of lime

Melt butter in a medium-sized frying pan and cook garlic for 1 minute. Add scallops and cook for 3–4 minutes on each side (depending on thickness of scallops) or until flesh is opaque and firm. Remove from pan and squeeze fresh lime juice on before serving.

363. Recipe—Coconut Rice and Sea Scallops

1 lb. sea scallops, rinsed and patted dry

3 Tbsp. fresh tarragon

3 Tbsp. fresh thyme

1 tsp. minced garlic

½ tsp. salt

¼ tsp. pepper

¼ cup olive oil

Place all ingredients except scallops into a bowl and mix. Add scallops, covering all sides of scallops with the mixture. Bake in 9x13 baking dish at 425°F on the second rack of the oven for 12–14 minutes.

Coconut Lime Sauce: Combine ⅔ cup cream with 4 tablespoons shredded coconut, 2 teaspoons yellow curry paste, juice of 1 lime, and 2 tablespoons of sugar in a saucepan. Cook over medium heat until thickened to a thin gravy consistency.

Rice: Cook rice according to package directions. We like brown rice with this dish and use 2 cups rice to 4 cups water. After rice is cooked, add 1 cup cooked frozen peas and carrots, 2 tablespoons chopped basil, and 2 tablespoons chopped thyme.

Plate as follows: rice mixture on plate followed by a drizzling of coconut lime sauce and top with sea scallops.

364. Fact—Every Valentine's Day I go all out and have a formal sit-down dinner. This year I made lobster, crab, scallops, and shrimp. Believe it or not, I bought enough for 4 servings for $34.93. (Lobster tails $4.99 ea., Snow crab $4.99/lb., medium shrimp $3.99/lb., large sea scallops $5.99/lb., and we even had enough shrimp leftover for another meal.)

365. Tip—Buy your seafood at New Year's and Valentine's Day and freeze it for later use. Typically you can purchase seafood between 25 and 50 percent off regular price during this time of year. *Make sure you freeze your seafood properly for long-term storage or you will be wasting your money!*

366. Tip—When buying live lobsters, watch them for a while to make sure they are active in the tank. If not, they may be ill.

367. Tip—If purchasing live shellfish, tap their shells. If they are alive, they will close their shells when tapped.

368. Tip—Never purchase mussels, clams, or oysters if they have cracked or broken shells.

369. Fact—According to the FDA, fresh seafood and fish can be safely refrigerated for 2 days.

370. Tip—When purchasing fresh fish and seafood, remember to freeze it if it will not be eaten within two days.

371. Tip—Here's how to freeze fish and seafood: Wrap fish in freezer paper, eliminating as much air as possible. My father was an outdoors man, and he would take our clean cardboard milk containers and fill them half full of water. He would then slip the fish, duck, or other meats in the water and freeze it. Later in the day when the water had turned to ice, he would fill the container to the top with water. We never had problems with freezer burn. The meat was obviously protected from air—it was encased in ice! You can also do this in freezer bags.

372. Tip—To freeze lobster, crab, and shrimp, I remove all air from the freezer bag and then wrap the bag with freezer paper. I also request frozen lobster tails, crab, and shrimp from the butcher shop. As soon as I am home I quickly wrap the packages in butcher paper, label and date them, and immediately place them in the freezer.

373. Fact—If properly frozen, lobster and other crustaceans will last 9–12 months.

374. Tip—Glaze fish to decrease freezer burn. Glazing fillets is a slow process, but I recommend it if you do not have a chest freezer and want to store fillets. What you do is dip a frozen fillet in ice-cold water and allow it to freeze by placing it on a cookie cooling rack covered with waxed paper. Repeat this process until ¼ inch of ice has formed on the fish. Wrap, label, and store as you normally would any frozen food.

375. Fact— Fish with high fat content do not freeze well and are prone to rancidity over time. Common fish containing higher levels of fat include rainbow trout, some salmon, herring, and mackerel.

376. Tip—I grew up in Redding, California, and we had a seafood market in town called Buzz's Crab Stand. I started learning at the age of 16 how to cook seafood from Buzz's workers. I would drive down to Buzz's and buy seafood to experiment with. My poor family has always been my culinary guinea pigs. Anyway, here's what Buzz's taught me about cooking clams, mussels, and oysters: Watch for the point at which their shells open; this means they're done. And remember to always discard ones that don't open.

377. **Tip**—To maintain the ocean-fresh taste of lobster, crab, mussels, and other seafood, cook in well-salted water.

378. **Tip**—Steam 1 pound lobster tails for 10 minutes or boil 1 pound lobster tail for 8 minutes. Always check that the meat is cooked before serving, even if the shell has turned red. Raw lobster meat is translucent; cooked meat is white.

379. **Fact**—When it was crab season, we ate Dungeness crab from Humboldt Bay several times a week. Our family would sit around the dining room table talking and cracking crab shells. We would put the cold crab meat on crackers followed by a drizzle of dressing. It was delicious! The dressing consisted of ketchup, Miracle Whip, and a splash of Worcestershire sauce. If you haven't eaten crab cold, you are really missing out.

380. **Fact**—Dungeness crab is low in fat.

381. **Tip**—I save crab and lobster shells and sauté them in butter. Remove the shells and freeze the butter for when you are ready to make another seafood entrée. This butter gives the seafood dishes I make a delicious and rich seafood flavor.

---

382. **Recipe**—Seafood Scallop Pasta

1 cube butter

1½ Tbsp. minced garlic

½ medium onion, chopped

¾ tsp. salt

¼ tsp. pepper

2 (6.5-oz.) clams, including juice

1 Tbsp. tarragon, minced

1 Tbsp. thyme, minced

1 Tbsp. oregano, minced

1 cup heavy cream or half-and-half

¼ cup water

2 Tbsp. corn starch

4 king crab legs

1 lb. mussels (I buy the half shell ones that are pre-steamed)

½ lb. medium shrimp, shelled, deveined, and steamed

2 Roma tomatoes, chopped

¼ cup basil, chopped

4 servings of cooked angel hair pasta

½ cup coarsely grated Romano cheese

Melt butter in a large pan and sauté garlic and onions until tender. Add salt, pepper, clams and juice, tarragon, thyme, oregano, and cream. Mix corn starch with water and add to mixture. When thickened, add mussels, shrimp, and crab legs. Simmer for 5 minutes. Add chopped Roma tomatoes. I serve this in large individual bowls. Place pasta in bowl followed by seafood mixture (make sure everyone gets some mussels and 1 crab leg) garnish with fresh basil and grated Romano cheese.

You may think this is expensive because of the seafood, but last time I made seafood scampi was June of 2011, and the seafood was $5.99 for a pound of half-shelled mussels, $2.50 for the medium shrimp, and $11.00 for four king crab legs. Total fresh seafood cost: $19.49—that's less than what a meal deal costs us for a family of four at a fast food restaurant, and it took only 20 minutes to fix.

383. Tip—When I serve crab or lobster, I encourage my family to wear cooking aprons at the table. The aprons protect their clothes from wayward sauces and yummy flying debris. Yes, eating shelled foods, such as crab and lobster, can become a little messy.

384. Tip—When eating messy seafood, provide warm, moist wash cloths at each place setting. I put ours, rolled up, on small plates to the left of the dinner plate. Guests and family are always appreciative.

385. Tip—Never eat the internal organs of a crab or any of the green stuff from the cavity. When my father taught me to shell a crab, he said, "The green stuff will make you sick; it's not fit for human consumption!" So when Dad wasn't looking, I tasted some. It tasted like bile, and I promptly spat it out and vowed that Dad was right; the green stuff isn't fit for human consumption!

386. Tip—For succulent cooked crab or lobster, cool for 5 minutes before serving.

387. Tip—For more information on lobsters, go to http://www .lobsterfrommaine.com.

388. Recipe—Seafood Stew

3 tsp. minced garlic

2 onions, chopped

4 stalks of celery, chopped

1 bell pepper, chopped

1 (8-oz.) can tomato sauce

2 (14.5-oz.) cans diced tomatoes

¾ cup concord grape juice

1 cup chicken broth

8 oz. clam juice

2 Tbsp. oil

1 bay leaf

1 tsp. oregano

½ tsp. cayenne pepper

1 tsp. salt

½ tsp. pepper

½ tsp. ginger

zest of one lemon

2 Tbsp. lemon juice

½ lb. clams

½ lb. mussels

1 lb. precooked seafood mixture (I buy a marinara mix)

½ lb. shrimp

2 (6.5-oz.) cans of clams, including juice

½ cup fresh chopped basil

In a large pot, sauté garlic, celery, onion, and bell pepper until tender. Add all ingredients except seafood and basil. Simmer for 10 minutes. Add clams and mussels. In 5–10 minutes, the clams and mussels will open their shells; this means they are cooked. Add seafood mix, shrimp, and canned clams and simmer for 5 more minutes. Ladle into soup bowls, making sure that each bowl has a fresh clam and mussel in it. Garnish with fresh basil. Serve immediately for best flavor. Makes 8 large portions.

389. Fact—The Seafood Stew is actually an inexpensive meal. Regular prices for the precooked seafood mixture is $2.99, a half pound of shrimp is only $2.50, and I bought the mussels and clams for $5.99 (½ pound of each). Total cost for the seafood: $11.48. When I buy it on sale, it is even less expensive.

390. Fact—Sometimes I make this soup with whippers that my husband catches at Willard Bay. I also add 2 cans of clams and 1 pound of precooked medium shrimp, and I have a delicious meal that is ready in 20 minutes for around $6.00 in shrimp and clams.

391. Fact—According to the FDA, some people are at greater risk for food-borne illness and should not eat raw or partially cooked fish or shellfish. These susceptible groups include: pregnant women, young children, older adults, persons whose immune systems are compromised, and persons who have decreased stomach acidity.

392. Fact—According to the FDA, pregnant women can avoid contracting a food-borne illness called *listeriosis* by avoiding refrigerated types of smoked seafood except in a cooked recipe, such as a casserole. Refrigerated smoked seafood, such as salmon, trout, whitefish, cod, tuna, or mackerel, is usually labeled as "nova-style," "lox," "kippered," "smoked," or "jerky" and can be found in the refrigerated section of grocery stores and delicatessens. They should be avoided. You needn't worry about getting listeriosis from canned or shelf-stable smoked seafood.

393. Fact—Advice from the FDA: if you are pregnant, nursing your child, or thinking about becoming pregnant, it is important that you avoid consuming too much methylmercury. This substance can be found in certain fish, and it can harm an unborn child's developing nervous system if eaten regularly. Don't eat shark, swordfish, king mackerel, or tilefish. However, don't deny yourself or your unborn baby the nutritional benefits of fish—you can eat 12 ounces (2 average meals) a week of other types of cooked fish as long as you eat a variety of fish that are low in mercury. This same advice should be followed when you're feeding fish and shellfish to your young child, but of course serve smaller portions.

394. Fact—The FDA recommends eating seafood that are low in mercury. These include shrimp, canned light tuna, salmon, pollock, and catfish.

395. Tip—A great website for keeping abreast of fish consumption advisories is hosted by the US Environmental Protection Agency: http://www.epa.gov/hg/advisories.htm.

396. Tip—Ever wonder how many shrimp are in the 1-pound package you bought at the market? Well, here's how to read a shrimp bag: count 21/25 means there will be between 21 and 25 shrimp in the bag.

THE PARABLE OF THE HUMBLE MOUSE

Once upon a time when animals could talk, there was a small brown mouse that lived in a meadow with a deer, a rabbit, a duck, a beaver, and a wise old owl. One summer's day while Humble Mouse was hanging her morning wash out to dry, Wise Old Owl quietly flew by. "Good morning, Wise Old Owl," Humble Mouse hollered up to her friend. Puzzled at seeing her night-time friend out during the day, Humble Mouse continued, "Shouldn't you be in bed sleeping?" Wise Old Owl looked lovingly down at Humble Mouse as he circled overhead, "I am gathering my food for winter. If I were you, Humble Mouse, I would prepare now while food is plentiful and easily found, for a harsh and early winter is at hand. I must leave now, my little friend, because winter waits for no one!" As Humble Mouse watched Wise Old Owl fly into the distance, she thought to herself, "Wise Old Owl has never led me astray. If he is preparing for an early winter, I should too. I am going to start my winter food storage today."

As soon as Humble Mouse had hung her last stocking on the clothes-line, she set off in search for food that would last her family through the winter. In no time at all, she found a plot of wild wheat. "What luck! This wheat will make my winter's bread." A few yards farther, Humble Mouse saw a large oak tree that had a branch heavy-laden with acorns. Humble Mouse looked up at the oak tree and smiled as she thought about the delightful acorn soup she would make for her family when the winter winds blew. Humble Mouse climbed up the trunk of the large oak tree, scampered across the branch, and plucked an acorn. Taking great care not to drop the acorn, she skillfully navigated her way across the branch and down the trunk of the tree without missing a step. Once on the ground and slightly out of breath, Humble Mouse cracked open the acorn and delicately nibbled its sweet meat. "I am so blessed! All of these acorns right here in the meadow. I must tell my friends so that they can be prepared for winter too." Off Humble Mouse ran to tell her friends Darlene Deer, Rachel Rabbit, Daniel Duck, and Beverly Beaver.

In no time at all, Humble Mouse ran into Darlene Deer, who was grazing on a patch of sweet clover.

"Darlene Deer! Darlene Deer! Wise Old Owl told me today that we are going to have an early winter this year. I have found some golden wheat and an oak tree not far from here that is full of sweet, ripe acorns. Let's go gather some so that we will be prepared for winter."

"Silly Humble Mouse, can't you see that I am eating this lovely patch of clover? Besides, I don't much believe in winter food storage, my parents stored food for the harsh winters that *other* Wise Old Owls prophesied about, and you know what? Those winters never came! And all my parents got out of it was less space, lost time, and spoiled food that had to be thrown out," sneered Darlene Deer as she turned her back to Humble Mouse and took another bite of the succulent clover. Saddened by Darlene Deer's bitterness and lack of concern, Humble Mouse scampered off in search of Rachel Rabbit.

As Humble Mouse was ambling down the path toward the briar patch where Rachel Rabbit made her home, she heard something quacking, "What are you doing this fine summer's day, my little friend?" There under the shade of a lilac bush was her feathered friend Daniel Duck. Smiling and using her most enthusiastic voice, Humble Mouse answered, "Hello, Daniel Duck! Wise Old Owl told me today that winter will come early this year. I have found some golden wheat and an oak tree not far from here that is full of sweet ripe acorns. Let's go gather some so that we will be prepared for winter." Daniel Duck waddled over to Humble Mouse, put his wing around her shoulders, and quacked, "I would love to join you, Humble Mouse, but today I am busy preparing for a family vacation in San Juan Capistrano. My cousin Sammy Swallow will be leaving for Argentina soon, and I want to see him before he leaves for the winter. I'll be returning in a few weeks—let's get together then!" And off Daniel Duck hurriedly waddled, not even waiting for Humble Mouse's reply. Feeling alone and a bit downhearted, Humble Mouse continued down the path to Rachel Rabbit's house.

When Humble Mouse arrived at Rachel Rabbit's door, she took a big, deep breath, smoothed out her apron, and firmly knocked on the door. A burst of commotion soon broke loose from behind the door. Humble Mouse could hear what sounded like a herd of buffalo trying to open the door, followed by loud voices crying out, "It's my turn to answer the door." "Get off my tail." "Stop pulling my ears." "I'm telling Mom." Finally, the commotion quieted down, and a disheveled white-and black-spotted, lop-eared rabbit with twinkling eyes opened the door and exclaimed, "My goodness, come in! Come in! It is so good to see you. What do I owe this surprise visit to, Humble Mouse?" Humble Mouse cleared her throat, stood up as tall as she could, and began, "Wise Old Owl told me today that winter will come early this year. I have found some golden wheat and an oak tree not far from here that is full of sweet ripe acorns. Let's go gather some so that we will be prepared for winter." Rachel Rabbit thoughtfully looked around her modest home and said, "I would love to, but Robert hasn't dug us a bigger burrow, yet and as you can see, we hardly have room for what we already have. And besides, even if we had a bigger burrow, how would I find time with all of the running around I do? Honestly, Humble Mouse, Molly has soccer practice three times a week, Lolly has ballet twice a week, and Polly has swimming lessons every day, and the schedule goes on and on!"

Humble Mouse carefully surveyed Rachel Rabbit's home and then timidly suggested, "Well, maybe you could store some acorns under the bunnies' beds or perhaps in the closets or maybe behind the sofa." Rachel Rabbit nervously laughed and replied, "No. No. That would never work. I'll start my winter food storage when I have a bigger burrow and more *time!*" At hearing yet another rejection from her friends, Humble Mouse, with her head hung low, slowly stood and made her way out the door of the burrow. Seeing the discouragement in Humble Mouse's countenance, Rachel Rabbit added, before closing the door, "You know, the Beavers might be interested. I hear Beverly's husband just added a new addition to their lodge." Hearing the news that Beverly Beaver had room for a winter's worth of food storage renewed Humble Mouse's hope, and off she scampered toward the pond to share her food storage find.

In no time at all, Humble Mouse was at the edge of Paradise Pond.

"Beverly! Beverly! Are you here?" sang out Humble Mouse's voice.

"Over here, Humble Mouse. I am here by the cattails." Humble Mouse scurried over to where the cattails were rustling near the water's edge. Beverly Beaver continued, "Do keep your voice low." "What are you doing that is such a big secret?" questioned Humble Mouse. Beverly Beaver smugly replied, "Humble Mouse, I am picking cattails for a secret facial cream I learned about in this month's issue of Beautiful Beaver Magazine." Beverly Beaver extended her paw and admiringly looked at her perfectly polished nails and continued with a sigh and a hint of irritation, "What do you want, Humble Mouse? I haven't got all day to chat. Beauty doesn't wait for anyone."

Humble Mouse felt a little insecure when she saw Beverly Beaver's freshwater pearl necklace and her perfectly manicured nails. Stammering, she rehearsed her message, "Wise Old Owl told me today that winter will be harsh and will come early this year. I have found some golden wheat and an oak tree not far from here that is full of sweet ripe acorns. Would you like to go with me to gather some so that we will be prepared for winter?" Beverly Beaver stopped looking at her nails and stared at Humble Mouse for what seemed to be minutes.

"Well, I certainly can't do that today, my dear. I have too many important engagements." Beverly Beaver climbed from the water's edge with a few cattails in her arms, looked Humble Mouse straight in the eye, and with a condescending tone said, "You just don't understand. I have a hydro-facial at noon and a tail waxing at 4:00. No! No! I certainly do not have time for such nonsense; besides, animals like me will always be able to buy anything we need at Meadow Market. They are open year-round, you know." Feeling inferior and embarrassed, Humble Mouse quietly crept away while Beverly Beaver examined her sleek fur coat for any signs of mud from her clandestine activities. Just when Humble Mouse believed she was out of sight of Beverly Beaver, she heard; "Humble Mouse, darling, you won't tell anyone about what I have been doing? Will you?" Humble Mouse shook her head as she replied, "No, Beverly Beaver. Your beauty secrets are safe with me."

Feeling low in spirits, Humble Mouse let out a big sigh and thought, *I guess it is up to me to prepare my family for winter.* And off she scampered to gather as many kernels of wheat as her apron would carry. After filling all of the bottles she owned with wheat, Humble Mouse moved on to harvesting her winter supply of acorns. As she strolled down the path toward the big oak tree, she thought to herself, *I should see if my friends have time to prepare for winter now.*

Once again, Humble Mouse made the journey to each of her friends' homes and just as before, not one of her friends cared to prepare for winter. Darlene Deer was grazing, only this time it wasn't clover, it was alfalfa. Daniel Duck was planning a vacation to the Caribbean. Rachel Rabbit said Robert still hadn't gotten around to digging a bigger burrow, and Beverly Beaver, though she had room for winter food storage, was more interested in spending her time getting a tummy tuck than on preparing things to put into her tummy.

Day after day, Humble Mouse gathered acorns until she had enough to make it through the winter. After stacking the last acorn in her attic, Humble Mouse said to herself, "Hum, now that I have the basics, I can focus on desserts. I think that a nice raspberry cobbler would warm our spirits on a cold winter's day." Tapping her chin with her pointer finger, Humble Mouse thought and thought of where she had seen some raspberries. "I know! I saw some along the banks of the brook." Humble Mouse grabbed her basket from the shelf, and as she stepped outside in search of raspberries, a gust of brisk wind chilled her to the bone. Taking her coat out of the closet, Humble Mouse shivered and said to herself as she buttoned up, "It's only the end of September, and it's this cold! Maybe Wise Old Owl is right. Maybe we *are* going to have an early winter."

Humble Mouse once again thought of her friends, "I should probably stop by and see if they would like to join me." Humble Mouse once again took the time to stop by each of her friends' homes; and once again Darlene Deer had no interest in preparing for winter, Daniel Duck was leaving on yet another vacation, Rachel Rabbit's bunnies' schedules still hadn't lightened up nor had Robert gotten around to digging a bigger burrow, and to top it off, Beverly Beaver wasn't even home—she was off getting her teeth whitened. Eventually Humble Mouse found and picked raspberries until her basket was filled to the rim. Once at home, Humble Mouse began to dry her raspberries so that they would last through the long, dark hours of winter. That night, as Humble Mouse got ready for bed, she smiled to herself and felt a little bit better about the arrival of winter.

In the morning, Humble Mouse looked out of her kitchen window and saw nothing but white! Humble Mouse shouted for her husband, "Henry, come quickly, something is covering our window!" Henry jumped out of bed and ran downstairs with such a start that he didn't even take time to put on his slippers. Staring at the window in disbelief, he ran to the front door, and when he opened it, he discovered a wall of snow! Henry turned to Humble Mouse, gave her a hug, and said, "I am glad I married a mouse who was smart enough to listen to Wise Old Owl's words of warning. Now how about a slice of whole wheat bread topped with raspberry jam to start our morning?"

When Darlene Deer woke up, she could not believe her eyes. She tried and tried to find something to eat, but no matter how long or how hard she pawed the snow, she could not uncover a single bite of clover. After giving her bleak situation some thought, she announced, "I know, I will go find Daniel Duck. He can fly and will surely be able to spot something for us to eat from the sky." Soon Darlene Deer found Daniel Duck, but he was flopped over on his side in a snow bank.

"Daniel Duck, what's wrong," asked Darlene Deer as she bounded to his side. Daniel Duck quacked back with labored effort, "I have been flying around the meadow all morning, and there is nothing to eat!"

"Let's go find Rachel Rabbit. She will certainly have a full pantry. After all, she has all of those bunnies to take care of," Darlene Deer said desperately.

"Good idea. But I'm going to have to waddle, for my wings are too tired to fly," panted Daniel Duck as he tried to right himself.

On the way to Rachel Rabbit's house, the two very hungry and tired beggars saw in the distance the big oak tree.

"I see the oak tree where Humble Mouse gathered acorns! Quickly, waddle faster!" demanded Darlene Deer. When the two arrived at the oak tree, much to their disappointment, its branches were bare. At seeing the bare branches, Daniel Duck seethed, "Would you look at that! How greedy! Humble Mouse didn't leave even one acorn for her friends!" Darlene Deer did not respond. She simply pressed on in search of the briar patch where Rachel Rabbit lived.

After what seemed to be hours, the two hungry friends met up with Rachel Rabbit and her bunnies.

"What are you doing here? Why aren't you at home eating lunch?" quacked Daniel Duck. Rachel Rabbit hesitated and then whispered so as not to alarm her bunnies, "There is no food to eat at home. I have told my bunnies that we are going to go on a hike before lunch; but in fact, I am looking for the brook so that my bunnies can fill their hungry tummies with the raspberries that Humble Mouse told me about." Daniel Duck's eyes widened, and with excitement, he quacked, "I know where the brook is. It's right around the bend!" With renewed hope, the hungry, tired, and very cold beggars trudged through the snow. Unfortunately, when they came to the brook, they discovered that all of the raspberries were gone. Daniel Duck was fuming and once again began blaming Humble Mouse for her greediness in picking all of the acorns and raspberries. When Rachel Rabbit heard Daniel Duck's disparaging comments about Humble Mouse's character, she pointed her paw at him and said sternly, "Daniel Duck, must I remind you that Humble Mouse invited us all to join her? And if you ask me, I think the bears came and finished off the raspberries, not our friend Humble Mouse! See those tracks?" The entire party gathered around, and sure enough, the raspberry patch had been besieged by bears.

"What are we going to do now?" moaned Darlene Deer.

"I know. We can follow the brook to Paradise Pond and ask Beverly Beaver if she can share some food. After all, with all of her wealth, she certainly will have food to spare!" replied Rachel Rabbit.

"Great idea!" quacked Daniel Duck.

"I bet her pantry is full of golden wheat, sweet ripe acorns, and delicious raspberries. Oh, I can just about taste them!" sang out a salivating Darlene Deer as she bounced about in the snow with excitement. The little party had walked only a few yards when they heard Beverly Beaver crying by the water's edge. Rachel Rabbit quickly hopped to her side and gently asked, "What's the matter, dear?" Sobbing, Beverly Beaver cried, "I am so hungry. We have no food. I went to Meadow Market, but a sign on the door read, 'Sold Out. See you next spring.' What am I to do? I can't eat my money. My money is worthless!" Much to everyone's surprise, Daniel Duck did not blame Humble Mouse this time. Instead Daniel Duck said, "We will go and find the wheat. Surely we will be able to find enough kernels to make a little bread."

Hours passed as the noisy little band of weary, hungry, and very cold beggars slogged through the deep snow in search of wheat. As they searched, they complained about the early winter. They complained that Wise Old Owl should have known the exact day winter would come. They complained that they were hungry, and they complained that they were cold and so very tired. Soon their steps became stumbles and their complaints turned to mumbles as one by one they collapsed in the snow and drifted off into an everlasting slumber. At last the meadow was quiet. Well, except for Humble Mouse's home, where laughter and pleasant conversation were enjoyed as the family gathered to eat a lovely winter's meal of warm wheat bread, acorn soup, and raspberry cobbler.

397. Recipe—My Favorite Whole Wheat Bread Recipe

5 cups hot water

½ cup oil

⅔ cup honey

2 Tbsp. liquid lecithin

7 cups whole wheat flour (you will need a total of 12–13½ cups)

1 Tbsp. dough enhancer

1 Tbsp. gluten

2 Tbsp. yeast

2 Tbsp. salt

Place all ingredients in a large bowl and mix for 5 minutes. Stir in 5–6½ more cups wheat flour and knead for 5 minutes. In a warm location, allow to rise in an oiled bowl covered with plastic wrap for 30 minutes. Cut dough into thirds and shape. Place dough into greased pans and bake in a cold oven at 350°F for 45 minutes or until bread has a hollow sound when thumped. Remove bread from pan and place on cooling rack. If soft-crusted bread is desired, spray with water or brush with butter. Try your hardest to wait 30 minutes before slicing.

398. Recipe—Acorn Soup

(As you may have guessed, I don't have an actual acorn *nut* soup recipe to match the parable, so I played on words and developed an acorn squash soup recipe that you are sure to enjoy on a winter's eve.)

3 cups acorn squash, cubed and cooked

2 Tbsp. oil

1 tsp. garlic

½ cup sweet red bell pepper, chopped

1 onion, chopped

½ cup mushrooms, sliced

4 cups chicken broth

1 cup Roma tomatoes, diced

juice of 1 lime

salt and pepper to taste

1 bay leaf

Cut acorn squash in half and scrape clean. Place upside down on a cookie sheet lined with aluminum foil and bake for 45 minutes. When squash is nearly finished cooking, heat oil and cook garlic in a large pot for 1 minute. Add red bell pepper, onions, and mushrooms, cooking until tender. Cube squash flesh and spoon from outer shell. Place all ingredients in cooking pot and heat to desired temperature.

399. Recipe—Raspberry Cobbler Recipe

(I use this cobbler recipe with any kind of fruit.)

1 cup flour

1½ tsp. baking powder

½ tsp. salt

½ cup sugar

1 cube butter, melted

½ cup milk

1 tsp. vanilla

¼ tsp. almond extract

3 cup raspberries

⅔ cup sugar

1 Tbsp. tapioca (if you don't have tapioca, use flour)

Preheat oven to 350°F and grease an 8x8 inch pan. Combine first four dry ingredients in a medium bowl. Add butter, milk, and vanilla and almond extracts. Stir only until blended. Pour into prepared pan. In another bowl, combine raspberries, sugar, and tapioca. Allow to set for 5 minutes and then spoon fruit mixture over batter. Bake 45–55 minutes or until center is set. We serve ours with vanilla ice cream.

QUICK MIXES

400. Recipe—Homemade Rice-a-Roni Mix

2 cups rice

1 cup spaghetti noodles, broken into 1-inch pieces

1 Tbsp. dried onion

2 tsp. parsley

½ tsp. ground ginger

½ tsp. garlic powder

½ tsp. salt

¼ tsp. pepper

4 cubes chicken bouillon

4 cups water

¼ cup butter

Melt butter in a large pan. Add rice and spaghetti and brown. Add remaining ingredients and simmer for 45 minutes with lid on pan.

401. Recipe—Cake Mix or Muffin Mix Cookies

1 cake mix or muffin mix

½ cup melted butter

2 eggs

Mix, scoop, and bake for 8–10 minutes at 350°F.

(Two of our family's favorite variations are yellow cake mix with butterscotch chips and coconut, and dark chocolate cake mix with mini chocolate chips.)

402. Recipe—Pancake Mix

8 cups flour

¾ cup dehydrated shortening

¾ cup powdered milk

¾ cup white sugar

⅔ cup dehydrated whole eggs

⅓ cup baking powder

2½ tsp. salt

Mix ingredients and store in an airtight container in a cool place. When ready for pancakes, just combine 1 cup pancake mix to 1 cup of water. Let stand for 2 minutes and ladle onto a hot, oiled griddle. Makes 6 four-inch pancakes.

403. Recipe—Brownie Mix

5 cups sugar

3⅓ cups flour

1⅔ cups oat flour

1¼ cups cocoa

½ cup + 2 Tbsp. dehydrated shortening

⅓ cup dehydrated whole eggs

1 Tbsp. baking powder

½ tsp. cream of tartar

¼ tsp. baking soda

1¼ tsp. salt

Mix ingredients and store in an airtight container in a cool place.

When you are ready to make brownies mix 3 cups brownie mix, ¾ cup water, 1 tsp. vanilla, and ½ cup chopped nuts. Bake in a greased and floured 8x8 inch pan at 350 degrees for 30 minutes. Cool slightly, frost if desired and cover.

404. Recipe—Muffin Mix

8 cups flour

2½ cups brown or white sugar

1¼ cups dehydrated shortening

½ cup powdered milk

⅓ cup baking powder

1½ tsp. salt

Mix ingredients and store in an airtight container in a cool place. When ready to make muffins, combine 3⅛ cup muffin mix and 2 cups water. Bake at 425°F for 20 minutes.

405. Recipe—Onion Soup Mix

⅔ cup dried onions

½ cup beef bouillon granules

½ cup dehydrated butter

2 Tbsp. cornstarch

2 tsp. onion powder

2 tsp. parsley flakes

Mix ingredients and store in an airtight container in a cool place.

406. Recipe—Chocolate Chip Cookie Mix

5⅓ cup flour

1⅓ cup oat flour

2 cups brown sugar

2 cups white sugar

2 cups dehydrated butter

¼ cup dehydrated whole eggs

2 tsp. baking powder

2 tsp. baking soda

1 tsp. salt

Mix ingredients and store in an airtight container in a cool place. When ready to make cookies, combine 2 cups chocolate chip cookie mix with ⅓ cup water, 1 teaspoon vanilla, ½ cup chocolate chips, ¼ cup nuts. Bake at 375°F on a greased cookie sheet for 10–12 minutes.

407. Recipe—Cheese Sauce for Mac-n-Cheese

6⅔ cup dehydrated cheese

1¼ cups powdered milk

1¼ cups dehydrated butter

1¼ cups flour

2½ tsp. onion powder

Mix ingredients and store in an airtight container in a cool place. When ready for cheese sauce, combine 1 cup hot water with ½ cup cheese sauce. Bring to a boil, stirring constantly.

408. Recipe—Sugar Cookie Mix

6 cups flour

3 cups sugar

2¼ cups dehydrated butter

1 cup oat flour

3 Tbsp. dehydrated whole egg

2 tsp. baking powder

1½ tsp. salt

1 Tbsp. cream of tartar

Mix ingredients and store in an airtight container in a cool place. When ready to make cookies, combine 2 cups mix with ¼ cup water and 2 teaspoons vanilla. Stir and form into a ball and roll out on a lightly floured counter and cut into shapes. Bake at 350°F 8–10 minutes.

To make snicker doodles, roll dough into 2-inch balls and dip into a cinnamon-sugar mixture. Flatten dough and bake at 350°F for 8–10 minutes.

409. Recipe—Cookie Mix for Peanut Butter Cookies

6 cups flour

1¾ cups white sugar

1½ cups brown sugar

1 cup + 2 Tbsp. dehydrated shortening

3 Tbsp. dehydrated whole eggs

2 tsp. salt

1¼ tsp. baking soda

Mix ingredients and store in an airtight container in a cool place. When ready to make cookies, combine 1 cup mix, ⅛ cup brown sugar, ¼ cup peanut butter, ¼ cup water. Shape into balls then flatten with a fork. Bake at 325°F for 10–12 minutes.

410. Recipe—Corn Bread Mix

5 cups wheat flour

5 cups corn meal

1⅓ cup dehydrated butter

¼ cup powdered milk

3⅓ cups brown sugar

½ cup powdered egg white

2½ tsp. baking soda

2½ tsp. baking powder

2½ tsp. salt

Mix ingredients and store in an airtight container in a cool place. When ready for corn bread, combine 3 cups mix with 1 cup water. Pour into a 8x8 greased pan and bake for 20 minutes at 350°F.

411. Recipe—Box Cake Mix

7 cups flour

5¼ cups sugar

1¾ cups dehydrated shortening

⅓ cup powdered milk

3 Tbsp. baking powder

2 tsp. salt

Store in an airtight container in a cool place. When ready to make cake, combine 5 cups mix with 2 eggs, ¾ cup water, and 1 teaspoon vanilla. Bake in a greased and floured 9x13 pan for 30–40 minutes.

412. Recipe—Sweetened Condensed Milk

6 cups sugar

6 cups powdered milk

1½ cups dehydrated butter

Store in an airtight container in a cool place. Combine 1⅛ cups mix with ¼ cup boiling water in food processor. Makes 14 ounces.

413. Recipe—Hot Cocoa Mix

5 cups powdered milk

½ cup cocoa

2½ cup powdered sugar

¾ tsp. salt

5 heaping tablespoons of mix to 1 cup of hot water.

Saving on Clothing

414. **Tip**—Buy your clothes at the end of the season.

415. **Tip**—Make shorts out of pants that have frayed hems.

416. **Tip**—Before purchasing clothing, make sure the fabric doesn't require expensive care such as dry cleaning.

417. **Tip**—Hunt down the discount rack at department stores.

418. **Tip**—Check out clothing at thrift stores and consignment shops; on occasion you will find new or nearly new clothing at significantly reduced prices.

419. **Tip**—Don't assume that discount clothing shops and thrift stores have lower prices than department stores.

420. **Tip**—Check out yard sales, especially for infant clothing.

421. **Tip**—Form a neighborhood closet for infant clothing.

422. **Tip**—Wear your clothing more than once. Some days I wear my jeans a couple days before laundering.

423. **Tip**—Teach your children to change into their play clothes after school and church.

424. **Tip**—Save stained clothes for camping, yard work, or painting.

425. **Tip**—Learn to mend your clothing. In 2010, I saved nearly $400.00 by sewing on buttons, mending holes, and repairing torn-out seams, as opposed to just replacing the clothes.

426. **Tip**—If you have a needle or straight pin that is having difficulty going through the fabric, run it along a bar of soap a few times or use a bar of soap for a pin cushion.

427. **Tip**—Spend the money on shoe polish, cork glue, weather proofing spray, or any other maintenance products you might need for your shoes. They really do increase the life of your shoes.

428. **Tip**—Teach children to hang up their clothing, not throw it on the floor or in the laundry basket. Laundering when not necessary wastes your time, electricity, gas, detergent, and water and will wear out clothing faster.

429. Tip—Check out the boys department for pants for all your kids. Oftentimes you will find unisex clothing for less in the boys department.

430. Tip—Recycle clothes; for instance, an older brother's dress shirt can be made into a night shirt for a little sister. All you have to do is add some lace or appliqués.

431. Tip—If you are just starting a family, save your children's clothing for the next child. Just label boxes with the sizes, and when the next child grows into the size, take it down from the rafters or from under the bed.

432. Tip—If you find some clothing with a mark at the bottom of a blouse that will be tucked into a skirt, ask for a discount. Most clerks are authorized to take 10 percent off a damaged purchase.

Saving on Groceries

433. Tip—Nurse your baby. It's less expensive, more healthful than formulas, and appears to reduce the risk of breast cancer in mothers.

434. Tip—If you can't nurse your baby, purchase powder formula over pre-mixed formula; it is usually less expensive.

435. Tip—To get a deal on fresh meats, find a grocery store that is closed on Sunday; come Monday morning, meat is usually marked down.

436. Tip—Eat less. Yes, you read right! Eat less. Portion sizes have increased over the years. For more information, read "Do increased Portion Sizes Affect How Much We Eat?" http://www.cdc.gov/nccdphp /dnpa/nutrition/pdf/portion_size_research.pdf.

437. Tip—Plan meatless meals a few times a week. Grains, beans, and legumes, along with fresh fruits and vegetables, make delicious, nutritious, and usually less expensive meals.

438. Tip—Purchase fruits and vegetables that are in season, never imported.

439. Tip—Shop farmers markets and eliminate the middle man.

440. **Tip**—Select less expensive cuts of meat (beef brisket, chuck steak, and round steak) and learn how to cook them (braise or stew) so they are tender. Here are a few examples: chicken breast versus chicken legs or thighs; ground hamburger versus asking the butcher to grind some less expensive meat that is on sale into "hamburger."

441. **Tip**—Find where your grocery store puts discounted meats. *Word of warning: sometimes those meats are not a good price in comparison to advertised meat specials.*

442. **Tip**—Buy your chicken whole and cut it up yourself. Here's how:

Rinse and dry chicken. Place on cutting board, breast up, with the legs facing you.

Pull the leg away from the chicken breast and slice through the skin. You will see where the thigh is attached to the breast.

Place the leg flat on the cutting board and slice, in one swift motion, through the meat and the joint.

Repeat on other side. Use same technique for the wings.

Firmly hold the chicken breast and slice from the pointy end of the breast where it attaches to the cavity. This will separate the breast from the back of the chicken.

Turn the chicken breast over and cut down the middle of the breast. You will now have two halves of breast.

You may further cut each half into smaller portions if desired.

443. **Recipe**—I use this coating for homemade chicken tenders for my "faux" Applebee's oriental chicken salad. My family actually likes my version better. Here is what you need: lettuce, green onions, matchstick carrots, red cabbage, almond crusted chicken tenders, mandarin oranges, crunchy Chinese noodles, and poppy seed dressing. Directions: wash and cut salad vegetables; toss in a large bowl. Slice cooked almond crusted chicken tenders into bite sized pieces. Plate as follows: tossed salad fixings, Mandarin oranges, chicken pieces, and crunchy noodles followed by dressing.

444. **Tip**—Make hamburger go further by adding healthful fillers such as oatmeal, barley, wheat, or even bread or cracker crumbs.

445. **Tip**—Join a co-op and receive volume discounts.

446. Tip—Plant a garden. In 2010 our garden, which consists of square-foot gardening and some fruit trees, saved us $2,505.29 in grocery expenses.

447. Tip—Raise chickens for eggs. We have 5 laying hens, and over 1 year they have laid 103.41 dozen eggs. The cost of crumbles, grit, corn, and straw was $151.56 (this doesn't include the electricity in the winter for their water heater). If I were to pay $2.99 a dozen for cage free, store-bought eggs, I have saved $157.64 by raising my own laying hens in 2010. By the way, using my husband's chicken coop design requires only 1 hour of chicken maintenance a week.

448. Fact—When I purchase a watermelon, I always keep my receipt. It if is bitter, I take it back and get another one for free.

449. Fact—Most produce managers will cut a melon in half for no additional charge. This gives you the opportunity to make sure it smells sweet and looks ruby red.

450. Tip—I have found that smaller strawberries tend to be sweeter than the larger ones. At our home we opt for flavor, not looks.

451. Tip—When whipping cream is inexpensive (50 percent off during the holidays), buy some, whip it, mound it on wax paper, and place it in the freezer. Once frozen, place whip cream mounds in an airtight container. When you are ready for hot cocoa garnish, pull one out of the freezer.

452. Tip—Always shop alone. Do not go with children, husbands, or even friends.

453. Tip—So that everyone is happy with the menu, ask each family member for at least one meal idea for the week.

454. Tip—Make a menu and stick to it.

455. Tip—When buying a large amount of bulk food, ask for a discount. Most stores will offer a 5–10 percent discount. Recently I bought a box of apples, which is about 40 pounds of fruit; I thought I would ask for a discount, just for the heck of it, and to my surprise they reduced the price by 6 percent.

456. Fact—If you don't ask for a discount, you definitely won't get one!

457. Tip—Use what you have in your pantry. Store what you eat and eat what you store!

458. Tip—Plan your weekly menu by using the *loss lead* items (items that lead you into the store because they are being sold at a loss) found on the front page of the weekly advertisement.

459. Tip—Don't ever shop hungry!

460. Tip—Use a shopping list.

461. Tip—Join your local grocery store's saver's club.

462. Tip—Don't cruise the aisles. Stay on the perimeter. Prepared foods are always more expensive. There are some savvy grocery stores that are beginning to play with this sage advice. They are actually moving prepared snack foods to one side of the perimeter; good for them, bad for you.

463. Tip—Use coupons for items you regularly use. I personally use very few food coupons because we mostly eat fresh foods that rarely have coupons.

464. Tip—Calculate if a deal is a deal. Packaging and unit prices can be deceiving. Use a calculator and figure out the price per count or ounce.

465. Tip—Try store brands; some I actually prefer to national brands, but for other products I always buy national brands because they really do taste better.

466. Tip—Check store websites for e-coupons.

467. Tip—Ask if stores price match. If so, be sure to have a copy of the ad they will be matching.

468. Tip—Know your prices, and when there's a good deal, stock up.

469. Tip—Learn the sales cycle for the grocery stores you shop at; for instance, March is the least expensive time to purchase cabbage and corned beef. Purchase a few extra for the freezer and enjoy corned beef throughout the year.

470. Tip—Check the discount shelves in grocery stores as well as department stores.

471. Tip—Find the day-old bakery shelf. Most day-old products are satisfactory and sell for 25–50 percent less.

472. Tip—Don't forget to ask for rain checks if an item is sold out. I learned this the hard way when I was told that a shipment was to come in the day before the ad expired. The shipment never came in, and I didn't think to ask for a rain check.

473. Tip—Check prices as the clerk scans them. Sometimes there are errors.

474. Tip—If a sign has a different price than the register reads, show the clerk the sign, and they will give you the posted price.

475. Tip—Check your receipt before you leave the store to ensure your bill has been properly credited for rebates and coupons.

476. Tip—I place impulse items in the child's seat of the grocery cart, and before I start placing items on the counter, I look at them and determine if I really need or want them. If I decide against the purchase, I politely tell the grocery clerk that I have changed my mind. The first few times I did this, I felt uncomfortable. Why? I don't know. I have always been treated politely, and now I do it without as much as a second thought.

477. Tip—Don't be loyal to your store. If the majority of your food items are on sale at another food chain, go to that grocery store.

478. Tip—I don't recommend driving all over town to save a nickel when it costs you $5.00 in gas. Be sensible about your time and money.

479. Tip—Make your own cookies, cakes, bread, hot cereal, granola, and so on. You will save money. In 2010 I baked three loaves of bread a week. We eat one loaf a week. The recipe start to finish takes 1½ hours. I saved $471.64 in one year by making our family's bread.

480. Recipe—Homemade Yogurt

> 1 gallon 2%, whole, or reconstituted powdered milk*
>
> 5 Tbsp. powdered milk
>
> 1 cup plain yogurt
>
> sweetener of choice

Preheat oven on warm setting. Place milk in a large, thick-bottomed, stainless steel pot and heat milk to 180°F, stirring often. Turn off oven and turn on oven light. Once the milk has reached 180°F, cool to

125–110°F. (I place the pot in a sink full of ice water; in 5–10 minutes the milk cools between 125–110°F.) Stir in yogurt, powdered milk, and sweetener.** Pour into pint-sized canning jars and cover with a canning lid and ring or aluminum foil. Place filled jars in oven and allow ripening in oven to desired consistency. I ripen mine 4–6 hours. Place yogurt in refrigerator. Makes 5 quarts of yogurt.

Yogurt will keep in refrigerator for a good 4 weeks. Remember to save 1 cup of your homemade yogurt as a starter for your next batch.

*Do not use ultra-pasteurized milk or yogurt will not set.

**I sweeten my yogurt by adding ¾ cup organic fructose to 1 gallon of milk. You may choose to add more or less sweetener depending on your preferences. I add the fructose with the powdered milk.

481. Fact—By making my own yogurt, I saved $122.44 in 2010.

482. Fact—By making my own cream cheese, buttermilk, and sour cream, I saved $63.89 in 2010.

483. Fact—By buying a half a beef, I saved nearly $1,200.00; and even when comparing advertised specials, I averaged saving 50 cents a pound on ground beef and roasts!

484. Fact—Most children want bakery goods from the store because of the decorations.

485. Tip—Purchase decorations at dollar or toy stores and save a bundle. You can also purchase fancy decorations from bakeries, or restaurant and cooking stores.

486. Tip—Restaurant equipment stores are inexpensive places to purchase your kitchen equipment and baking supplies.

487. Tip—If you want cold cereal, wait until September when most cereal companies and grocery stores offer incredible deals. Also save your coupons for this time, and you will save even more and sometimes pay nothing at all!

488. Tip—Store-bought, premade cookie dough is expensive. Try making a triple batch of cookie dough at home and freeze the individual cookies on a cookie sheet. Once frozen, place in an airtight container. When you are ready for fresh-baked cookies, defrost and bake as many as you want.

489. Fact—Raw cookie dough increases the risk of salmonella. To eliminate this risk, pasteurize your fresh eggs or purchase pasteurized eggs in the refrigerated section of your grocery store. (See fact 841 to learn how to pasteurize eggs.)

490. Tip—Buy expensive grocery items, such as seafood, only when on sale.

491. Tip—If you fill up your car with gas once a week, buy your milk then too. Milk at gas stations typically is cheaper than grocery store prices.

492. Tip—Buy canned goods during case lot sales; however, only purchase foods your family will eat. If you aren't eating what you store and storing what you eat, you will lose money when it expires and you are forced to throw it into the trash bin.

493. Tip—Buy soda and chips that your family likes rather than those that they love. My family tends to not gobble them up as quickly when I do this.

494. Tip—When buying produce, check to see if the per pound price is really more expensive than the pre-bagged price.

495. Tip—If the pre-bagged price for fruits is less expensive, make sure the fruit is of equal quality; that is, they are fresh and show no signs of mold, bruising, and so on.

496. Tip—Smaller, individual fruits are often less expensive than their larger counterparts.

497. Tip—Remember that some fresh items can be frozen. Here's an example: I really like one brand of fresh pasta that a local grocery store carries; however, the price is up there, so I don't buy it until it is near the expiration date and is significantly reduced. Every week I check to see if it is reduced. When I find that it has been reduced, I buy all that are marked down. We eat one package for dinner, and then I freeze the remaining packages.

498. Fact—Believe it or not, sometimes prewashed and cut vegetables are less expensive than bulk.

499. Fact—Some prewashed, ready-to-eat foods have led to food-borne illness outbreaks. Wash even prewashed foods for safety.

500. **Tip**—I buy my candy the day after a holiday. By doing this, I save 50 percent on candy. And I don't know about you, but my children don't care if the candy wrapper has holly on it in January; they care about what's inside.

501. **Tip**—I buy my seasonal decorations, wrapping paper, picnic supplies, and so on at the end of the season, thereby saving 50 percent or more. It doesn't bother me that I am one year behind the times.

502. **Fact**—Grocery stores often have specials that are coordinated with national holidays or annual food promotion months. For instance, the best time for BBQ items is near Father's Day. The best time to stock up on frozen food items is during the frozen food month. By the way, frozen food month is March.

503. **Fact**—*Sell by* date, *use by* date, and *best if used by* date all have different meanings. USDA FSIS define them as follows:

"Sell-By" date tells the store how long to display the product for sale. You should buy the product before the date expires.

A "Use-By" date is the last date recommended for the use of the product while at peak quality. The date has been determined by the manufacturer of the product.

A "Best if Used By (or Before)" date is recommended for best flavor or quality. It is not a purchase or safety date.

504. **Tip**—For more information regarding food product dating and storage, visit http://www.fsis.usda.gov/factsheets/food_product_dating/index.asp.

Saving on Transportation

505. **Tip**—Take a class at a community center or community college on how to change your car's oil.

506. **Tip**—Fill your car fluids and change the filters yourself. You can purchase the fluids and filters on sale and not pay for labor.

507. **Tip**—Invest in a tire pressure gauge. Under- or overinflated tires decrease gas mileage.

508. **Tip**—Have your tires rotated according to schedule.

509. Tip—Read your manual and follow the maintenance guide. Checking problems before they affect other parts saves money and time.

510. Tip—Get your brakes changed before they wear out or you will be paying for expensive rotors.

511. Tip—Exchange your services with those of your mechanic. For example, you can watch your mechanic's children four times for four hours so he can take his wife out on a date, and he in return can rotate your tires and change the brake pads. Be sure to pre-arrange the monetary value of each other's skills so that there will be no loss of friendships or hurt feelings.

512. Tip—Carpool to work and for errands.

513. Tip—Plan out your errands so that you're taking the most efficient route, thereby saving time and gas money.

514. Tip—Book airplane travel in advance and track the least expensive days of the week to purchase tickets. Some airlines have lower prices on Tuesdays and Wednesdays.

515. Tip—Consider taking a train or bus. I took the train once from California to Oregon in the winter, and the scenery was magnificent.

516. Tip—Buy a motorcycle or moped to get around.

517. Tip—Walk or bike instead of drive. I bought an adult tricycle a few years ago for $500.00. This adult bicycle has a huge basket that can hold all of our family's groceries, dry cleaning, mail, hardware purchases, and so on. I spent $3,827.20 in 2009 on gas for my car, not including vacations; after using my tricycle for most of my errands in 2010, I spent $1,472.00 on gas. This is a savings of $2,355.20 in gas! If I were to multiply this savings by the 3 years I have had my tricycle, I have saved $7,065.60 in gas; not bad for a $500.00 investment. My tricycle not only saves my budget, but it also helps the environment and gives me exercise to boot!

518. Tip—Drive the speed limit.

519. Tip—Don't abruptly stop or race the engine by accelerating quickly from a stop.

520. Tip—When using public transportation, check out special rates for students, elderly, children, and disabled patrons.

521. Tip—If you are using public transportation, be sure to ask for transfer stamps.

522. Tip—If you are using public transportation, determine if monthly passes will save you money.

523. Tip—If you are not going to be using an automobile for an extended period of time, weigh out the risk of removing it from your automobile policy. We did this when our truck blew an engine and we knew it would sit until spring. By doing this, we saved $286.97.

524. Tip—Apply for good student discounts, even when in college. It saved our daughter who is in law school $50.00 a month.

525. Tip—Study your auto insurance policy. We get free assistance when we run out of gas. They will actually bring us enough to get to a gas station. If we break down, we have free towing. We also have free rock chip repairs, and should we lock our keys in our car, the locksmith charges are free. Because nothing is without a price, I asked if opting out of these benefits would lessen our premium, and to my surprise, it wouldn't.

526. Tip—Shop around and save coupons for windshield replacement. I called our insurance company and discovered that I could save more money and get a factory windshield by using a coupon at an "unauthorized" local windshield repair shop. The fact of the matter: I saved $92.00 on one car and $106.00 on the other by not going to the windshield repair shop my insurance recommended.

SAVING ON ANIMAL CARE

527. Tip—Go to your local feed store for vaccines.

528. Tip—Shop around for prices on spaying and neutering. Animal shelters and neutering clinics often have the best deals around. However, don't depend on these clinics for all of your services; most animal shelters and neutering clinics do not treat injured or sick animals.

529. Fact—Many neutering clinics also provide vaccines and microchipping at reduced prices.

530. Tip—Ask for a multiple pet discount. Typically it will save you 10 percent if you bring all of your animals in at one time.

531. **Tip**—After shopping around for animal services I saved nearly $1,000.00 in 2010. These savings were on dental cleanings, heart worm prevention, spaying of two dogs, lab work, X-rays, shots for 4 puppies, and vaccines for 2 adult dogs and 2 adult cats.

532. **Tip**—It is less expensive to have your pet's teeth cleaned on a regular basis than to pay for fillings, antibiotics, or an extraction. Preventive maintenance not only saves money but also eliminates unnecessary and painful conditions from developing in your pet.

533. **Tip**—We no longer take our dogs to the groomers. This saves us $65.00 a visit. By giving our dogs a bath and trim, we have saved $1,119.00 a year.

534. **Tip**—You may think that shelter adoptions are high priced, but after considering the costs of an examination, vaccines, spaying or neutering, and microchipping, you will soon realize you are getting a tremendous bargain.

Entertainment, Dates, and Vacations for Dollars a Day

535. **Tip**—Theaters and orchestras: Purchase tickets in performance bundles or buy season tickets.

536. **Tip**—Theaters and orchestras: Many plays have reduced prices for opening nights.

537. **Tip**—Theaters and orchestra: Some theaters discount unsold tickets the day of the performance.

538. **Tip**—Theaters and orchestras: For Broadway plays, consider buying from a ticket broker.

539. **Tip**—Theaters and orchestras: Check for discount tickets offered by community sponsors, such as grocery stores, banks, and department stores.

540. **Tip**—Theaters and orchestras: Ask for student discounts, military discounts, and professional discounts.

541. Tip—Theaters and orchestras: Attend high school productions; they are less expensive and very enjoyable.

542. Tip—Theaters and orchestras: Attend college productions and community theater groups and orchestras. The price is a bargain, and the talent is wonderful.

543. Tip—Theaters and orchestras: Want to see a play or enjoy a symphony for free? Volunteer to usher.

544. Tip—Movies: Check the prices at all movie theaters showing the same movie you want to watch. Where I live, ticket prices vary by $3.25 a ticket for the same show seen the same day and time of night.

545. Tip—Movies: Check out discount nights, such as date night, military discount night, or other specialty night. We went to a movie on Tuesday and saved $4.50 because it was date night. Who says a date has to be on the weekend?

546. Tip—Movies: Consider going to a matinee.

547. Tip—Movies: Buy a video and watch it at home.

548. Tip—Movie: Check out a movie for free at the community library.

549. Tip—Movie: Check out a movie from the college library.

550. Tip—Movie: In the summer, many communities throughout the United States offer free outdoor movies.

551. Tip—Movies: Borrow movies from friends.

552. Tip—Movies: Participate in summer movie programs for children. Theaters often have children summer movie clubs that offer $1.00 tickets.

553. Tip—Eating out: Ask for early bird specials.

554. Tip—Eating out: Go out for breakfast or lunch instead of dinner and you will typically spend less money for the same delicious food.

555. Tip—Eating out: Cook dinner at home and go out for dessert.

556. Tip—Eating out: Coupon, coupon, coupon!

557. Tip—Eating out: Order takeout and have a picnic in the park. This saves you 20 percent for a tip.

558. Tip—Eating out: Don't order a la carte. It ends up costing you $7.00 for a 50-cent potato.

559. Tip—Eating out: Ask the waiter if there are any specials.

560. Tip—Eating out: Sign up for free birthday lunches, dinners, and ice creams. My children have great memories of eating all day for free on their birthdays.

561. Tip—Eating out: Split an entrée and order a side salad and a dessert to share.

562. Tip—Eating out: Rethink why you are eating out. Is it for a great meal, service, not having to do the dishes? If it is for a little pampering, why not form a dinner group consisting of four couples. Each couple will take turns hosting an all-inclusive (my term for not asking guests to bring anything or do the dishes) dinner at their home once every three months. By following this schedule, each couple will host three times a year and get to enjoy a lovely meal without the work or expense the other 9 months.

563. Tip—Eating out: We reduced our "eating out" dates from four times a month to once a month and saved $1,950 in 2010.

564. Tip—Think outside of the box. Have friends over for a movie or game night. Also rethink your menu. Who says you have to serve elaborate, fancy, or expensive foods? Remember your friends are coming to enjoy your companionship.

565. Tip—Sporting events: Look for discount tickets offered by corporate sponsors.

566. Tip—Sporting events: Check websites for discounts and e-coupons.

567. Tip—Sporting events: Check out farm stores for discount rodeo tickets.

568. Tip—Sporting events: Community league, college, high school, and even little league ball games can be lively, entertaining, and keep you on the edge of your seat for a lot less than professional games.

569. Tip—Sporting events: Ask if they have "locals" discounts.

570. Tip—Sporting events: Why rent a tennis court when you can use community courts and high school courts for free?

571. Tip—Sporting events: Ask about family ticket packages and professional discounts.

572. Tip—Sporting events: See if there are less expensive days to attend; for example, one local ski resort has family night skiing, where a family can night ski for $40.00 on Monday nights.

573. Tip—Recreation: Look into buying entertainment activity cards. Trent and I bought one for $50.00, and we can ski, play miniature golf, and even go to professional baseball games throughout the year on predetermined dates, all for less than one lift ticket would cost.

574. Tip—Recreation: Go to the lake or a drive in the mountains.

575. Tip—Recreation: Go camping.

576. Tip—Recreation: Buy a national or state park pass.

577. Tip—Recreation: Go on a bike ride or hike and have a picnic.

578. Tip— Recreation: Stargaze and roast marshmallows.

579. Tip—Vacation: check if local annual memberships to entertainment venues such as the zoo or planetarium have sister associations with other venues that you may visit in other cities. We have received discounts ranging from free admissions to discounts on food and gift shop purchases.

580. Tip—Vacation: Before traveling, find out if your local bank or credit union has a reciprocal agreement with other financial institutions for ATM fees.

581. Tip—Vacation: Find out if your auto insurance policy covers rental cars before purchasing extra insurance through the car rental agency.

582. Tip—Vacation: Price check to see if an all-inclusive deal is really a deal. For our lifestyle, it usually isn't.

583. Tip—Vacation: When buying excursions, look for deals. On our last vacation, we paid $57.00 for the same full day all-inclusive tour that others paid $132.00 for.

584. Tip—Vacation: Rent a house or condo instead of two hotel rooms. More often than not, it is less expensive, and you have more privacy.

585. **Tip**—Vacation: We almost always eat breakfast and dinner in the condo and pack a lunch and snacks to munch on while on vacation. To ensure I get a break from the kitchen, Trent and the children will each cook one dinner for the family.

586. **Tip**—While on vacation, run into local grocery stores for food items rather than convenience markets or hotel snack shops.

587. **Tip**—Typically we go out to eat dinner twice a week while on vacation. One night is "parents' date night," and Trent and I go out for some romance and fine dining, and the other night is "children's choice." The children get to select where they would like the family to eat dinner.

588. **Tip**—Vacation: Stay with family and friends.

589. **Tip**—Vacation: Join a house-sitting association and house-sit while you vacation.

590. **Tip**—Vacation: Use public transportation instead of rental cars and taxis.

591. **Tip**—Compare prices for foreign travel. Once while traveling in Europe, we saved money and time by flying instead of riding a train to our next destination.

592. **Tip**—Vacation: Look for professional discounts and coupons.

593. **Tip**—Vacation: Bring your own water bottle to the pool so you don't have to buy expensive poolside drinks.

594. **Tip**—Vacation: Purchase amusement park tickets through reputable online discount vendors. If you work for the government or another large company, see if they offer discount tickets to amusement parks.

595. **Tip**—Vacation: Check to see if amusement parks allow outside food and drinks; believe it or not, some do!

596. **Tip**—Vacation: Remember a vacation should be not only fun but also relaxing. You should plan some days by the pool. It's free and it's fun.

597. **Tip**—Vacation: Give each child their spending money and tell them they can keep what they don't spend. This cuts down not only on requests for money but also on frivolous and expensive but cheap souvenirs.

598. **Tip**—Vacation: Stay in the least expensive hotels that are clean and safe and have essential amenities. Many expensive hotels are expensive because they have fancy lobbies and a concierge. Let's face it, most children only care about the pool and pushing elevator buttons.

599. **Tip**—Vacation: To save up for vacations, I put aside any unexpected money I receive. I also tuck away any money that is under our budget; for example, if I have budgeted $50.00 for groceries and I spend only $45.00, I take the $5.00 and put it in the vacation fund. You will be surprised how quickly extra money accumulates.

600. **Tip**—Vacation: Plan a *staycation* and enjoy all of the local sites that you never took the time to see. It won't cost much because you can sleep in your own bed at night.

601. **Tip**—Vacation: Consider vacationing during the off seasons. You'll save money and not have to fight the crowds. I usually plan to go off season during the first week that the price is reduced so that if luck is with me, the weather will still be pleasant.

602. **Tip**—See if it is better to rent or own recreational vehicles. Sometimes it will actually save you money to own.

603. **Tip**—Check to see what the roaming charges will be if you use your cell phone out of the United States. I have paid up to $2.68 a minute and 50 cents a text.

MEDICAL BILLS AND AUTO BILL PAY

604. **Tip**—Price shop for medical care (physician care, pharmacy, hospital, and medical equipment suppliers, to name a few). When I was experiencing my first pregnancy, it was determined I would need a cesarean section. This was going to be a very expensive procedure for our family since my husband was self-employed at the time. I went to work finding out what the major charges would be at various hospitals. I couldn't believe the differences in rates. After I found the least expensive hospital, I then called my physician to see if he had privileges there. Fortunately, he did and we were able to save around $1,500 in hospital expenses. This has not been an isolated incident; a few months ago, I saved nearly $3,000.00 by hospital shopping. I always compare prices for medical care, and you should too.

605. Tip—Ask health-care providers if they offer uninsured discounts or sliding scale fee schedules based on income.

606. Tip—Ask health-care providers if they give discounts for cash payments. You'd be surprised how many will discount your bill 5–10 percent.

607. Tip—Check to see what hour the health-care facility begins charging for an additional day. Do everything in your power to be discharged before that time.

608. Tip—Don't forget personal toiletries; who wants to pay $12.00 for a box of facial tissues?

609. Tip—Understand your insurance coverage. You will save thousands of dollars by using preferred health-care providers and facilities.

610. Tip—Evaluate your medical cafeteria plan options and select only those services that meet your health-care needs and budget.

611. Tip—Evaluate your need and use of secondary insurance. When I was working fulltime, we discovered that my insurance was not a benefit because a third insurance policy was ineligible for medical payment. What did I do? I opted out of the insurance as soon as was possible and saw an increase in my take-home pay because I wasn't paying a premium for insurance I couldn't even use.

612. Tip—Compare insurance benefit packages offered by your and your husband's employer. One insurance may pay better as a primary insurance than a secondary insurance, thereby saving you money.

613. Tip—Evaluate insurance coverage options. Perhaps a plan with higher co-pays and deductibles will save you money in premiums and still meet your needs.

614. Tip—If you know that you will be meeting your deductible for the year after a hospitalization or surgery, postpone all elective treatments and procedures until after this date, and you will save money. This is especially true if two different households are using the same insurance policy for health-care benefits.

615. Tip—Enroll in a health-care savings account and use it!

616. Tip—Carefully examine your hospital bills. Once we were overbilled $658.00.

617. Tip—Ask for a co-pay discount if you pay upon admission to the hospital. I did and saved $175.00.

618. Tip—Ask for a discount if you pay your hospital bill in full. I did and was told they wouldn't discount my bill. I then asked if I would be charged monthly interest on any unpaid balance. They said no. I paid the minimum payment for 3 months. A few weeks later, I received a call from the hospital billing department and was offered a 20 percent discount if I paid my bill in full. I did, and my balance was reduced by $512.00.

619. Tip—Hospital bills aren't the only ones to overcharge; in 2010 I was overcharged $157.00 by the dentist, $32.00 by a physician, and $40.00 by a chiropractor. How did this happen? By billing personnel not sending claims to my secondary insurance. I discovered this when I didn't receive an explanation of benefits from my secondary insurance company.

620. Tip—File your explanation of benefit letters for each medical expense, and when all of the bills come flooding in, compare what your insurance has determined you should pay and what the medical providers say you should pay. I have actually had the medical providers bill me for more than the insurance plan allowance. Fortunately, all it took to reduce the charges was a photocopy of my explanation of benefits letter from my insurance.

621. Tip—Get second opinions if medical or dental examination results are unusual. I have had two experiences with dentists that were deserving of second opinions. The first was when my daughter was young and the dentist wanted to build her an expensive orthodontic appliance to help close the gap between her teeth. I questioned the appliance because most children seemed to have a natural closure of their two front teeth. He insisted that it wouldn't happen in her case, so I told him I would discuss it with my husband. What I did next was find an orthodontist who gave free consultations. He told me that her teeth were beautiful and would close on their own—and they did! The second experience occurred when we moved to a new town. We made an appointment with a local dentist, and he found numerous cavities in all of our mouths. I couldn't believe what I was hearing because we rarely had cavities in the past; so I scheduled an appointment with another dentist and much to my savings, the second dentist said our mouths were healthy and cavity free. When we received our bill from the first dentist, there was also an error. We were all charged for nitrous oxide yet my husband was the only one who used it.

622. **Tip**—When you have your yearly eye examination, ask for your prescription. I did and realized that both of my eyes were the same prescription, +1.50. This was a wonderful discovery because I was able to purchase 4 pairs of reading glasses for $19.99 at a major discount warehouse rather than paying $286.00 at the optometrist's office for one pair of reading glasses.

623. **Fact**—I do not use auto bill pay any longer. Why? Because I found hidden fees that I had to fight to get reversed. I also had renewal of services that were not authorized. And lastly, I had money taken out of my account twice in the same month because of an accounting glitch. Each of these examples was from a different company.

Gardening Tips

624. **Tip**—If you are paying for secondary water, you should be using it. Plant a square foot garden, plant a patio container garden, or if nothing else, use the water for house plants.

625. **Tip**—If you don't want to plant a garden but have the plot and secondary water, rent the plot out for someone else to garden.

626. **Tip**—I soak my peas and beans overnight in water before planting to speed up germination. Be careful not to soak them too long or they will split and not germinate.

627. **Tip**—If you are like me and don't like to wear gloves while gardening, try scratching your fingernails over a bar of soap so that soil can't get under your nails.

628. **Tip**—To scrub my hands clean after gardening without gloves, I use cornmeal, water, and bar soap.

629. Tip—After working all day in the garden without gloves, my hands need an extra boost of lotion. I apply a little glycerin followed by my hand cream or body lotion. If I have stains on my skin, I add 1 part lemon juice to 2 parts glycerin.

630. Tip—To battle aphids, combine 1 quart water with a ½ teaspoon dish soap and spray on vegetation.

631. Tip—The best time to pick vegetables is the morning before the sun has a chance to cause the slightest amount of withering.

632. Tip—Many grocery stores sell watercress with root systems attached. Cut off the leaves and use in your salad or soup. Now instead of composting the roots, plant them in the garden and grow your own watercress.

633. Tip—Go to garage sales to pick up garden tools. Many secondhand tools can be cleaned up and sharpened to be as good as new.

634. Tip—To find out what people are giving away for free, visit Free Cycle at http://www.freecycle.org/

635. Tip—If you want a garden tool to have a soft, squishy handle, cover it with foam water pipe insulation.

636. Tip—If your friend or neighbor has some plants that you admire, ask for a cutting, seeds, or bulbs.

637. Tip—Start a bulb and seed exchange in your community.

638. Tip—Start your seeds in the winter rather than buying plants in the spring. It is easy, fun, and economical.

639. Tip—The best time to water grass or the garden is in the morning so that plants are properly hydrated to take on those hot summer rays. Watering in the morning also decreases evaporation.

640. Tip—Always clean off your garden tools before putting them away to limit rusting.

641. Tip—If your tools tend to disappear during community projects, mark the handles with bright paint.

642. Tip—I use Epsom salts for my tomato plants. Use 1 tablespoon per foot of tomato plant height every 2 weeks.

643. Tip—For more tips on using Epsom salts, visit http://www.epsomsaltcouncil.org.

644. Tip—If you have garden tools with wooden handles that cause splinters, sandpaper the handles and apply some lacquer.

645. Tip—When I lived in Arizona, I would transplant my cacti using tongs.

LEFTOVER MAGIC AND MENU PLANNING

646. Fact—The key for successfully using leftovers is to disguise the shape, change the flavor, and if you can, freeze it and serve it the following week.

647. Fact—According to Business Insider, the average American consumer wastes 250 pounds of food a year. For more information, visit http://www.businessinsider.com/fao-wasted-food-2011-5.

648. Tip—Leftover roasted turkey can be used in turkey divan, turkey soup, or turkey pillows.

649. Tip—Leftover roasted chicken can be used in chicken noodle soup, chicken salad sandwiches, Hawaiian haystacks, chicken cacciatore, and oriental chicken salad.

650. Tip—Leftover roast beef can be used for BBQ sandwiches, sweet beef tortillas, roast beef sandwiches with au jus, and tostadas.

651. Tip—Leftover ham can be used in split pea soup, breakfast casserole, or lima bean casserole.

652. Tip—Leftover steak can be used in enchiladas, steak chili, tostadas, or steak salad.

653. Tip—Leftover hamburger can be used in stuffed bell peppers, marinara sauce, and soup.

654. Tip—Leftover baked fish can be used in fish cakes, fish sandwich spread, or seafood soup.

655. Tip—Leftover spaghetti can be made into a version of baked ziti.

656. **Tip**—Leftover mashed potatoes can be used in shepherd's pie, twice-baked potatoes, or potato soup, or as a thickener in soups.

657. **Tip**—Leftover steamed rice can be used in cabbage rolls, fried rice, soups, or rice pudding.

658. **Tip**—Leftover corn can be made into corn chowder, corn fritters, and corn salsa.

659. **Tip**—Left over asparagus can be made into asparagus soup.

660. **Tip**—Leftover vegetables can be made into omelets or quiche.

661. **Tip**—Leftover French bread can be used for bread pudding, stuffing, or french onion soup. Or make croutons by drizzling with garlic butter and then baking on a cookie sheet. You could also make a breakfast strata.

662. **Tip**—Leftover brownies and cookies can be used as ice cream mix-ins. I also break the leftovers into crumbs and freeze them to be used later to decorate cakes, pudding, or cheesecake crusts.

663. **Tip**—Leftover pound cake makes a delicious fondue dipper.

664. **Tip**—Make ice cream sandwiches with leftover cookies.

665. **Tip**—Leftover ice cream sundae fixings can be made into a Baked Alaska.

666. **Tip**—Whenever I make homemade pudding, I also make lemon meringue pie, angel food cake, or macaroon cookies to use up the egg whites.

MAKING OLD THINGS NEW AGAIN THROUGH RECYCLING

667. **Tip**—Have a white elephant Christmas, where family members draw names and then give previously owned gifts found in their closets or purchased at thrift stores. Give awards for the best buy, most unusual, or most creative gifts.

668. **Tip**—Make gifts from plant cuttings or seeds from your yard.

669. **Tip**—Take a basket from the attic and fill it with home-canned foods, a loaf of fresh bread, and freezer jam to give as a gift.

670. Tip—I use plastic grocery bags to pick up doggy doo in the backyard. It's quicker than scoopers and doesn't cost anything.

671. Tip—5-gallon ice cream buckets and honey containers make great treasure pails at the beach or forest.

672. Tip—5-gallon ice cream buckets also make wonderful kitchen compost pails. Be sure to keep the lid on or the scraps will attract fruit flies before you have a chance to dump it outside.

673. Tip—Need a smock for your child to paint in? Use one of Dad's old shirts! My mother did this when we were young, and it worked great.

674. Tip—Keep the plastic, zippered linen bags that sheets and pillowcases come in. I use them for a myriad of things, such as cosmetic bags, pillow storage, quilt storage, art supplies storage, and so on.

675. Tip—Feed leftover fruit, vegetables, and rice to your chickens. We even offer our dogs grains, fruits, and vegetables; they love them!

676. Tip—If you have little helpers in the kitchen, save the drink holders that you get at fast food restaurants; they are great for carrying drinks out to the patio without spills.

677. Tip—Use cardboard toilet paper rolls to keep ribbons and rope from becoming tangled.

678. Tip—Recycle old toothbrushes by using them as tile cleaning brushes. I also use them to scrub the soles of our shoes clean when they become muddy.

679. Tip—You can wash and reuse plastic picnic utensils.

680. Tip—Make children's mittens, vests, and beanies out of old sweaters. The edge of the sleeve is the wrist portion of the mitten. The bottom edge of the sweater bodice is the vest, and the neck of the sweater is the cuff of the beanie.

681. Tip—Use old day calendar pages and the backs of mailed envelopes for messages, memos, or grocery shopping lists.

682. Tip—When I get extra condiments with our fast food orders, I place them in the refrigerator and use them for picnics or brown bag lunches.

683. Tip—Recycle old candles by making new ones. Here's a fun activity to do with children:

Supplies and tools:

1 *cardboard* milk carton

old cooking pot

old candle

stove

coloring

1 tapered candle

ice cubes

Clean and dry the *cardboard* milk carton. In an old pot, melt wax from an old candle over medium heat. Once wax has melted, add coloring. Insert tapered candle and hold in place as you fill the milk carton with ice cubes. Remove your hands; the ice will hold the candle in place. Carefully pour melted wax into milk carton. Do not move the milk carton. Allow your candle to cool for two days. After two days, your candle will be solid. Drain off the water from the melted ice cubes. Carefully tear off the milk carton. Enjoy the fun shape of your candle. Candles need to cure for at least two weeks before they are burned or they will melt away.

684. Tip—When I bake cookies for a friend, I buy pretty plates at thrift stores. It adds a nice touch, and I don't ever worry about getting my plate back.

685. Tip—Reuse bakery boxes when you take cookies, cakes, brownies, or pies on a picnic or to a friend. They protect the baked goods and you don't need to worry about your plate.

686. Tip—Save old bedsheets and use as tableclothes at picnics.

687. Tip—Make body pillowcases and pillowcases from a torn bed sheet.

688. Tip—Top sheets can be used as draw sheets (a sheet to enable the moving of a person who is bed bound). All you do is fold the top sheet in half, lengthwise.

689. Tip—Speaking of sheets, ever struggle with folding a fitted sheet? Here's how:

Start with the sheet inside out, and slip your hands into the lengthwise mattress pockets.

Bring your hands together and turn the right pocket right-side out over the left pocket.

Smooth out the sheet and repeat with the lower pockets.

Do the same thing with the remaining pockets so that all four pockets are nested inside each other, and fold as you would a towel.

690. Tip—Take old terry towels and washcloths and cut them into 6-inch squares. Sew several of them together and add some ornamentation, and you have a new hot pad.

691. Tip—Once I somehow licked a postage stamp too much and it wouldn't stick. I couldn't find any glue, so I dried the stamp, applied some fingernail polish to the back side, and placed it on the envelope; it worked like a charm!

692. Tip—Chip canisters can be used to store crafts, bread crumbs, homemade croutons, or open bags of pasta. They also make a great container for care package cookies.

693. Tip—Newspaper agencies sell the ends of rolls of newsprint; these are great for covering picnic tables and for drawing and finger painting.

694. Tip—Plastic baby wipe containers make wonderful tubs for little odds and ends. Just label what's in them so you don't need to open 10 containers before you find what you want.

695. Tip—Another great storage container is an empty prescription bottle. It can be used for buttons, snaps, thumb tacks, paper clips, and even fishing lures and flies. Once again, label your containers or you will become very frustrated trying to find what you need.

696. Tip—A friend of mine had a sister who had very long hair. Guess what she used for hair curlers? Empty soup cans! She held the curlers in place with long metal hair clips.

697. Tip—Save sour cream, cottage cheese, yogurt, ricotta cheese containers, and similar containers to store leftovers. I do not recommend heating foods in any plastic container since plastic is not inert and will transfer more rapidly into foods when heated. To be honest, I am a fan of glass containers.

698. Tip—Need a squirt gun in the summer but don't want to run to the store? Try this: fill a well-rinsed dishwashing detergent bottle with water. It squirts better than any squirt gun I have seen.

699. Tip—When making punch, consider freezing some of the punch and fruit in a sour cream container or gelatin mold and then allowing it to melt in the punch bowl for a decorative and nondiluting alternative to ice cubes.

700. Tip—Use snagged knee-highs for a soap holder when camping. Place a bar of soap in the knee-high and tie around the water spigot. This works great on the garden spigot too.

701. Tip—Rather than buy a camping egg carton, I fill pint jars with eggs. This is the perfect amount of eggs for our family, and I don't have to worry about the egg shells being crushed because there aren't any!

702. Tip—Turn empty plastic containers and orange juice cans into freezer packs for ice chests by filling with water and freeing. This saves a little money but also uses the disposable packaging at least 1 more time if not more.

703. Tip—One year my son's teacher had the children make homemade Christmas ornaments by punching a partridge shape into a metal orange juice lid with a nail. They then glued satin ribbon around the edge and made a loop for the ornament hanger. I still hang it every year on our tree.

704. Tip—Recycle bows by applying two-sided tape to the bottom.

705. Tip—Make drums out of old cardboard oatmeal containers for your children. Be sure to allow the children to decorate them with construction paper, lace, beads, macaroni, and paints.

706. Tip—Make stilts out of old cans. Drill a hole in the side of the can near the bottom and another hole directly across from the first hole. Thread some rope through the holes and tie a knot. For more comfortable gripping, place the knot inside of the can. Repeat procedure on another can and now you have an inexpensive pair of stilts.

707. Tip—Old plastic one-pound strawberry containers are great for storing Lego building blocks.

708. Tip—When growing vegetables vertically, make slings for heavier crops out of used panty hose.

709. Tip—Old panty hose make great tethers for vine plants. They secure but won't dig into the plants.

710. Tip—I was taught this trick by my husband: to remove any sediment from paint, pour it through an old pair of panty hose stretched over a bucket.

711. Tip—Here's another painting trick: if you need to stop painting but haven't finished the job and don't want to take the time to wash your brush, try wrapping your brush in plastic wrap or placing it in a vacuum sealable bag.

712. Tip—For a fun family reunion game, place a grapefruit in one foot of a pair of panty hose and tie the other leg around your waste so that the grapefruit hangs 2–3 inches from the ground. Place another grapefruit on the ground (make two sets). Form two teams and have a relay race to see which team can knock their grapefruit to the finish line first using the panty-hosed grapefruit.

713. Tip—Another fun idea for family reunions is to make individual laminated place mats featuring copies of old photos and newspaper clippings from the lives of your relatives. Sandwich colorful paper, photos, and clippings between sheets of laminating film.

714. Tip—Save mesh fruit and vegetable bags for hanging garden vegetables in your basement cold storage space.

715. Tip—Mesh fruit and vegetable bags make great totes for beach toys.

716. Tip—Mesh fruit and vegetable bags are great for storing bath toys.

717. Tip—Use old cardboard egg cartons to make homemade fire starters. Combine saw dust and melted paraffin wax together to form a paste. Spoon the mixture into egg cartons and allow it to cool. When you need to start a fire, just break off an egg section of the carton, and you have a wonderful fire starter. Be careful not to heat the paraffin too hot because it is combustible.

718. Tip—Dryer lint makes a good fire starter too!

719. Tip—Make homemade postcards out of cereal boxes. One side of the box is a fun picture and the other side is for writing. Kids love making and receiving them!

720. Tip—Styrofoam meat trays can be cleaned and used for paint or glue palettes.

721. Tip—Styrofoam meat trays can also be used for protecting items to be mailed. Take two meat trays, make a clam shell around the item, and seal with tape.

722. Tip—To keep embroidery floss from tangling, my Grandma Garbett would cut cereal boxes and other thin cardboard into squares, notch the edges with v's, and then wrap the floss around the cardboard.

723. Fact—WD-40 claims there are over 2,000 uses for their product. Here's the website: http://www.wd40.com/uses-tips/.

724. Tip—Twenty-pound bags that once held dry dog food can be filled with trash.

725. Tip—Give old magazines to the art teacher or librarian at your children's schools.

726. Tip—Cancel magazine subscriptions; read library copies.

727. Tip—Request new books at your local library and ask that you be placed first on the waiting list to read them when they comes in.

728. Tip—Grow potatoes in discarded automobile tires.

729. Tip—Use a punctured bicycle tire tube and a plastic soda bottle to make a rocket. Here's how:

Supplies and tools:

1 bicycle tire tube

1 empty plastic 1 liter soda bottle

1 cork the diameter of the opening to the soda bottle

petroleum jelly

1 drill and bit the size of the bike tire valve

knife

Cut tire tube valve out of tube, leaving a ring of rubber connected to the valve. Save the tube; you can use this to make other fun projects.

Measure and cut the cork if necessary so that when the valve is inserted through the cork, the threaded portion of the valve will be visible and the opposite opening will be inside the bottle.

Fill the soda bottle ⅓ full of water.

In the center of the cork, drill a hole that is the diameter of the valve.

Lubricate the valve with the petroleum jelly and slide the valve into the cork. Place the cork into the bottle.

Build a launch pad. Find an open field and place the rocket on the launch pad.

Attach the bicycle pump to the rocket and begin pumping. When enough pressure has built up, the rocket will blast off!

CLEANING AND HYGIENE TIPS

730. Fact—By ironing my husband's shirts instead of taking them to the cleaners, I saved $774.80 in 2010.

731. Tip—The best time to have formal wear dry cleaned is right after high school prom because many dry cleaners offer specials around this time of year.

732. Tip—To freshen your house as you vacuum, place a few tablespoons of your favorite potpourri in your vacuum bag.

733. Tip—A seam ripper cuts through hair, dental floss, or string wound around the vacuum roller brush.

734. Tip—When applying liquid makeup, pour the amount you will be using onto the back of your hand; this reduces the chance of bottle contamination, thereby reducing the risk of pimples.

735. Tip—My favorite lip gloss is $12.99 a tube; I thought that was too much, so I now spend $2.99 for a tube of lip balm and apply it over my lipstick. The shine is subtle and my lips aren't as dry.

736. Tip—Instead of spending $14.99 for sun barrier, I buy zinc oxide from the drugstore for $1.99–$3.99 a tube. If you look at the active ingredients, you will see that zinc oxide is in the $14.99 tube as well. So if your nose and cheeks are fried and you still want to enjoy the sun some more, pick up a tube of zinc oxide and have some fun playing in the sun!

737. Tip—Another use for zinc oxide is to treat diaper rash. In fact, zinc oxide is a main ingredient for several brands of diaper rash ointment. Zinc oxide can be a bit thick and sticky for little bottoms, so I mix some glycerin or vitamin E oil in with it and it glides on.

738. Tip—There is about ½ an inch more lipstick in a tube below the top of the applicator. Rather than throwing the tube away when I can no longer glide it across my lips, I use a lip brush to get every last bit of lipstick out of the tube. This gives me 3–4 more months before I need to purchase a new tube.

739. Tip—For years I thought my mother was a redhead. One day I came home from college and she had brown hair. I actually asked her why she had colored her hair brown. You can imagine how surprised I was when she told me brown was her natural color. I asked her how she managed to keep her hair coloring a secret, and she said that one of her tricks was to apply petroleum jelly along her hair line so that the hair coloring would dye only her hair and leave no traces on her skin.

740. Tip—If you get a ring stuck on your finger, spray your finger with Windex and the ring will slip off.

741. Fact—Never mix ammonia or vinegar and bleach; toxic fumes are made.

742. Fact—Never mix bleach and cleansers such as Comet or Ajax; toxic fumes are made.

743. Tip—To make a homemade abrasive dry cleanser, combine 4 parts baking soda with 1 part borax.

744. Tip—Another good abrasive paste is salt, baking soda, and enough water to form a paste.

745. Tip—To prevent little helpers from over-sprinkling cleansers, cover half the holes of the powdered cleaner lid with masking tape.

746. Tip—Homemade window cleaner: 4 quarts warm water, ½ teaspoon dishwashing liquid, ½ cup vinegar, ½ cup rubbing alcohol.

747. Tip—Homemade windshield washing fluid: 3 cups rubbing alcohol, 10 cups water, 1 teaspoon dishwashing liquid.

748. Fact—Borax is a natural cleaner and is less toxic than most cleaners.

749. Tip—Borax can be used as a dry powdered cleanser for bathroom fixtures.

750. Fact—Borax is poisonous if ingested.

751. Tip—Dial Corporation's customer service phone number is 800-457-8739.

752. Tip—Add ½ cup of borax to your wash for cleaner clothes.

753. Fact—I used cloth diapers for my children except when we traveled.

754. Tip—I added ½ cup of borax to the diaper pail to reduce odors.

755. Tip—Many people are complaining about a white film on their dishes and glasses since dishwasher detergents have changed to a more environmentally friendly formula. If you want an inexpensive solution for this film, place ¼ cup of borax in the bottom of the dishwasher, and spots will be gone.

756. Tip—If you are breaking a lot of glasses in the dishwasher, place them at an angle and they will not break from expansion.

757. Tip—When washing stemware, line the bottom of your sink with a soft plush towel.

758. Tip—Never wash fine china in the dishwasher, especially if it has gold ornamentation.

759. Tip—Clean a blender or food processor the easy way by filling it with warm water and a few drops of dish washing liquid. Turn it on for a few seconds and rinse.

760. Tip—Turn dark clothes inside out to launder and dry and the colors will not fade as quickly from friction.

761. Tip—To minimize wrinkles, shake clothes before placing them in the dryer.

762. Tip—I take my clothes out of the dryer as soon as they are finished, place them on a hanger, give them a mist from a spray bottle filled with water, and then smooth them out with my hands. Often times I don't need to even iron them.

763. Tip—If your iron ever gets grungy on the bottom, just make a paste of baking soda and water and rub it onto the cold iron. Allow to dry and then rub off. (Do not use this method on irons with a nonstick bottom as it may be too abrasive.)

764. Tip—If I don't want to iron a shirt or skirt and it has light wrinkling I hang it in my bathroom, and after Trent and I have each showered, the steam has removed the wrinkles.

765. Tip—To remove mineral deposits from the inside of a steam iron, fill the water reservoir with vinegar, allow it to sit for 20 minutes, then steam an old rag with the vinegar steam. Repeat if necessary. After the iron is sufficiently cleaned of mineral deposits, fill the water reservoir with water and steam out any vinegar odors.

766. Tip—Use 1 cup vinegar in toilet bowls to disinfect. Allow to soak for a couple of hours and then scrub with a toilet brush.

767. Fact—Most people know that vinegar is made from alcohol and apples, but did you know it is also made from corn?

768. Fact—Growing up in Northern California meant lots of boating and swimming. It also meant many sunburns. My mother applied vinegar to our sunburns; it really does help take the sting out.

769. Tip—Baking soda is another option for cleaning a toilet bowl.

770. Tip—Never clean light bulbs while on. The cool moistened cloth against the hot glass will shatter the bulb.

771. Fact—Something that many people forget to clean is the range fan. You will be surprised how dirty it gets; especially if you cook a great deal with oils. I clean the mesh filter in my dishwasher.

772. Fact—Another item that is often neglected is the dryer vent hose. Check the vent hose for kinks and lint deposits. After removing lint, be sure to position the hose so that there are no kinks because lint can collect in those areas and create a fire hazard.

773. Tip—I have heard that full strength vinegar sprayed on dandelions and unwanted grass will kill them.

774. Tip—Sidewalk cracks can be filled with salt to eliminate weed and grass growth.

775. Tip—Here is a really cool tip for winter: mix 1 cup vinegar with 3 cups water and spray your car windows. In the morning, they will be frost free.

776. Tip—For more helpful tips using vinegar, visit the Heinz Vinegar website: http://www.heinzvinegar.com/.

777. Tip—Wall cleaner: ½ cup borax and 4 quarts warm water.

778. Tip—Wipe down your refrigerator and freezer shelves and walls with a mixture of 1 tablespoon baking soda and 1 cup water.

779. Tip—A good general cleaning solution is equal parts vinegar and water (use on baseboards, window ledges, and so on).

780. Tip—I clean my hard wood floors using 1 cup vinegar mixed with 4 quarts water.

781. Tip—Scrubbing the shower walls regularly with a vinegar solution will eliminate mildew without using harsh chemicals such as bleach. If you don't want to use vinegar, you may like ¼ cup borax, ¼ cup baking soda, and 1½ cups warm water.

782. Tip—To freshen up sink and shower drains, sprinkle 1 cup baking soda followed by 1 cup vinegar. Be sure to stop the drain so that the foaming action will stay confined to the drain. Allow to foam and then rinse with cool water.

783. Tip—When I laundered my baby's clothes, I always added a cup of vinegar to the rinse cycle to remove any lingering soap residue.

784. Tip—Pretreat tough clothing stains such as collar and perspiration stains with Fels-Naptha bar soap.

785. Fels-Naptha is typically found in the laundry product aisle in most grocery stores.

786. Fact—Sunshine will brighten white clothes.

787. Tip—If line-drying clothes, be sure to wash your clothes line to prevent soiling of clothing.

788. Tip—Hanging jeans by the pant legs will decrease wrinkles because of their weight.

789. Tip—Don't throw away citrus peels; use them to freshen up your garbage disposal.

790. Tip—When I was working as a nurse, I would occasionally get blood on my white uniform, and I found that the only way to get blood out was to pour hydrogen peroxide on the spot of blood repetitively until it foamed out.

791. Tip—Butter will remove most adhesives from shiny objects without damaging the finish.

792. Tip—Lemon juice will remove strong food odors from cutting boards and fingers.

793. Tip—½ cup lemon juice to 4 quarts of water makes a very good kitchen and bathroom counter cleaner.

794. Tip—To clean your copper-bottom pots and pans, cover the copper with salt, slice a lemon in half, and scrub the copper.

795. Tip—Vinegar will remove strong food odors from cutting boards and fingers.

796. Tip—Lemon juice will remove hard water spots.

797. Tip—Lemon juice will remove fingernail stains.

798. Fact—I saved $469.02 by not having acrylic nails and doing my own at-home pedicures. As it was, I only went to the salon for pedicures only 4 times a year, but the savings add up.

799. Tip—Vinegar will remove hard water spots.

800. Tip—Full-strength vinegar gently applied with a cloth will remove salt stains from leather shoes.

801. Tip—Clean chrome with a paste of cream of tartar and vinegar.

802. Tip—To clean discolored pots and pans, soak in 2 tablespoons vinegar, 1½ tablespoons cream of tartar, and 1 quart water.

803. Tip—Clean baked-on food from a microwave by placing water in a microwave-safe bowl and cooking on high for 2 minutes. In no time at all, the steam will soften the baked-on food, and you can wipe it away easily. To freshen up a microwave, add a little lemon rind or vinegar to the water.

804. Tip—For helpful uses for baking soda visit the Arm and Hammer website: http://www.armandhammer.com/solutions.aspx.

805. Tip—Apply dishwasher liquid (it must be the enzymatic formula—not the chlorine formula) to burned cookware and allow to set for an hour or two and baked-on foods will lift right off with no scrubbing necessary.

806. Tip—Freshen your car or any room in the house by sprinkling a few drops of a natural oil of your choice onto a cotton ball and placing it in an inconspicuous location.

807. Fact—Sometimes when I have scratches in my furniture and can't find the correct match for wood stain, I use a felt tip pen.

808. Tip—Learn how to remove common children's art products such as glue, paint, silly putty, and modeling clay by visiting http://www.crayola.com/canwehelp/staintips/guide.cfm.

809. Fact—One Christmas I made homemade gifts for my grandparents. My mother taught me how to make natural moth deterrents for clothes closets. You take an apple and stick whole cloves all over it. Then attach a satin ribbon to the apple using a florist staple. Apparently moths do not like cloves.

810. Tip—Here is another inexpensive but useful Christmas gift: Make homemade bath salts by mixing 1 tablespoon glycerin with a few drops of food coloring and essential oil, slowly drizzle over 3 cups of Epsom salts, and mix until salts are covered in color.

811. Fact—Over time, I get a build-up of hairspray on my bathroom wall. I clean it off by using a soft cloth and rubbing alcohol.

812. Fact—For shampoo build-up, I rinse my hair with 1 cup of vinegar, massage my scalp for a couple of minutes, and then rinse.

813. Tip—Remove gum from hair using peanut butter. It really does work, just ask my daughter Rachel who regularly fell asleep with gum in her mouth at night. Be patient and work the peanut butter through the hair.

814. Tip—When the toothpaste tube is empty, I cut my tube, starting from the end, and get 5 more days' worth of toothpaste out of the tube. No one else in the family will do this. Let's do some math, 5 days times 4 empty tubes equals nearly a month of toothpaste that was going to be thrown into the bathroom wastebasket. And if the tubes come from my children or husband, I get almost 10 or more days of toothpaste from their discarded tubes.

815. Tip—When my body lotion container is no longer pumping out lotion, I cut the container in two and get around 10 more days of applications from the container. Multiply 10 days by the four lotion containers in our house, and I get around 1 month of lotion that was just going to be thrown into the wastebasket! My family mocks me for being so cheap; but, I just never want to be without and feel guilty about what I threw away.

816. Tip—Freshen up retainers and dentures using 2 teaspoons baking soda in 1 cup of water. Rinse after soaking.

817. Fact—Once while I was camping I discovered I forgot my toothpaste. Gram taught me that baking soda can be used for toothpaste. Just wet your toothbrush and dab it into a little baking soda and brush as you normally would. The taste isn't very good, but my teeth felt clean afterward.

818. Tip—Gram also said that before they had deodorant she would make a paste out of baking soda and water. I haven't ever tried it, but I keep it tucked in the back of my mind just in case I need it in an emergency.

819. Fact—The main ingredient in most cuticle oils is mineral oil. Why pay a for a little coloring? I just put some mineral oil on a cotton ball and apply it to my cuticles.

820. Tip—Witch hazel is a must-have in my medicine chest. It costs about $1.00 and has multiple uses. It is a disinfectant and anti-inflammatory. I use it for cuts, scratches, bug bites, and pimples. If I get a pimple, I apply some witch hazel on a cotton ball to the site 3–4 times a day and in about 4 days, it's gone.

821. Fact—Speaking of bug bites, mosquitoes are attracted to dark colors, especially dark blue. Perhaps you remember the old movies where the safari men are wearing tan clothing. There was a reason; mosquitoes are not attracted to light colors. Trent didn't believe me, so we did a test, and guess what? Yup, he was a mosquito magnet in his blue jeans, and I hardly had any mosquitoes buzzing me in my tan jeans.

822. Tip—When outdoors, use straws in soda cans to prevent wasps from landing inside your soda can and stinging your lip. True story; it happened to me once on Whiskey Town Lake when I was a kid.

823. Fact—One of the main ingredients in most facial astringents is witch hazel. I make my own astringent by mixing 2 parts witch hazel and 1 part water.

824. Tip—In the winter, I don't use deodorant because I perspire very little; instead, I use the witch hazel astringent for my underarms.

825. Fact—Epsom Salt got its name from Epsom, England, where it was first discovered.

826. Fact—I used to do a little runway modeling when I was young, and we would place a little petroleum jelly on our finger and rub it along our teeth so that our lips wouldn't stick to our teeth. I did the same thing when I was a bride and stood in my reception line for hours. It really helps.

827. Tip—Keep perfume and cologne in the refrigerator to extend the life and prevent changes in the scent.

828. Fact—When my husband shaves and trims his facial hair, it falls into the bathroom sink, making cleanup difficult. I have found that by using a damp tissue I can get every last hair out of the sink with little effort.

829. Fact—Damp sponges pick up liquids better than dry sponges.

MISCELLANEOUS COOKING TIPS

830. Tip—Soaking bamboo skewers for 30 minutes before using will prevent them from burning. Covering them with aluminum foil helps too.

831. Tip—Because meat, vegetables, and fruits grill at different rates, I use three different skewers, one for the meat and one for the vegetables and fruits.

832. Tip—If you love BBQ corn on the cob that is served at amusement parks and want to make your own at home, here's how: pull husks down to the stalk of the corn, taking care not to remove the husk. Remove the silk, then add butter, salt, and pepper. Pull up the husk and tie the top closed with some cooking twine. Grill on medium-high heat for 15 minutes or until the kernels are cooked. Be sure to turn every 5 minutes so that your corn doesn't burn.

833. **Fact**—These days it is difficult to bring treats to children's classrooms, Sunday school classes, ball games, and so on because of food allergies. I thought about what I could take and came up with rice krispy treats. So far, knock on wood, not one parent over the years has said their child was allergic to them.

834. **Tip**—To keep rice krispy treats from sticking to your fingers when you press them down into the pan, moisten your hands with a little water.

835. **Tip**—I use an egg slicer to slice my strawberries for decorations. The slices are uniform and look so pretty when fanned open.

836. **Tip**—Here's how my gram made perfect poached eggs: Bring one quart water and ½ teaspoon salt to a simmer in a pan. Break the freshest egg you have into a small bowl or ramekin. Angle the bowl into the simmering water and allow the water to gently wash into the bowl and slip the egg from the bowl and into the water. Remove from heat. Cover the pan and let sit for 6–7 minutes or until whites of eggs are firm and yolks are covered with a thin, white film. Remove the eggs with a slotted spoon.

837. **Tip**—Gram also taught me that spicy dishes become more flavorful if one tablespoon of sugar is added.

838. **Tip**—Cabbage rolls require intact leaves; boiling the cabbage invariably results in torn and unusable leaves. To remedy this situation remove the core from a head of cabbage and wrap it in several layers of wet paper towels. Microwave on high for 10 minutes or longer depending on the size of the head. The leaves are easily separated. If you find that the inner leaves are not cooked and pliable, just wrap the cabbage in wet paper towels and repeat the process.

839. **Tip**—To substitute evaporated milk in a recipe requiring fresh milk, dilute evaporated milk by ½ with water.

840. **Tip**—Need to store a sliced onion but don't want to smell up the house? I put mine in a mason jar with the lid on and place it in the refrigerator.

841. Tip—How to pasteurize raw eggs: Place the room-temperature eggs in a colander and lower them into a pan or bowl of 142°F water. Put an instant-read thermometer in the bowl to make sure you have a high enough temperature and that it remains constant. If your eggs are medium or large, leave them in the water for 3½ minutes; for extra-large or jumbo eggs, leave them in for 5 minutes. When the time is up, remove the eggs, dry them, and refrigerate them in a tightly covered container. This tip is a must for raw cookie dough eaters or for Caesar salad dressing.

842. Tip—If it is Easter and you forgot to pick up an egg coloring kit, don't worry; just mix 1 tablespoon of vinegar into ½ cup of water and add 20 drops of food coloring. To make purple, add 5 drops of red and 15 drops of blue.

843. Tip—Brick cheese will mold faster if you touch it with your fingers while slicing. To remedy this, scoot the plastic wrap back, only exposing the amount of cheese you would like to use.

844. Tip—A quick way to remove cubes of avocado from the skin is to slice it in half and remove the pit. Then cut vertically and horizontally and use a large spoon to scoop the cubes out.

845. Tip—To easily remove skin from chicken, grab the skin with a paper towel and pull.

846. Tip—When breading meat, dredge in flour then egg then crumbs. Use one hand for dredging and the other for the egg mixture and only one hand will get covered in paste.

847. Tip—When boiling fresh beets, leave 2 inches of the beet top and all of the root and the color will not bleed out.

848. Tip—Don't discard beet tops; steam or sauté them as you would spinach.

849. Tip—Roll your lemons and limes on the counter with the palm of your hand before you juice them and you will get more juice.

850. Tip—I don't throw out wilted celery. I revive it by washing it and placing it in resealable bags.

851. Tip—If only using half of an onion, do not remove the skin of the half not being used. This will reduce the odor and prolong the shelf life.

852. Tip—To extend the shelf life of asparagus, cut about an inch off the bottom of the spears and stand upright in a glass filled with 2–3 inches of water and refrigerate.

853. Tip—To extend the life of melons, only scoop out the seeds of the half you will be serving. Leave the seeds in the other half, wrap with plastic wrap, and refrigerate.

854. Tip—To extend the life of lettuce, do not remove top leaves until ready to use.

855. Tip—To make crispy home-cut fries, soak fries in ice water as you cut them.

856. Tip—If your evening cookout is rained out before making S'mores, make them in the microwave. Place a graham cracker on a napkin followed by milk chocolate and then a marshmallow. Heat on high until the marshmallow swells. Remove from microwave and top with another graham cracker. Wait a while, and the chocolate will soften. Enjoy!

857. Tip—Never leave garlic preserved in oil at room temperature as it increases the risk for botulism.

858. Tip—Do not leave baked potatoes in aluminum foil as it increases the risk for botulism.

859. Tip—Don't wash fruit until ready to eat. Many fruits are coated with waxes to maintain freshness longer.

860. Tip—The trick for flaky pie crust is using chilled liquids.

861. Tip—Roll out pie crust between two sheets of wax paper so it doesn't stick to the countertop or rolling pin.

862. Tip—The trick for flaky buttermilk biscuits is keeping the butter cold while cutting into the flour.

863. Tip—To keep pie crust edges from burning, cover edges with strips of aluminum foil.

864. Tip—Keep cooked foods warm by covering them and placing them in the microwave. It is a small space, so the heat will dissipate and maintain the temperature of the food better.

865. Tip—To determine if cooking oil is hot enough to fry, place a 1-inch cube of bread in the oil, and if it is golden brown in 1 minute, the oil is ready.

866. Tip—If you have a burner catch fire from a spill, douse it with baking soda.

867. Tip—If you suspect you have become ill from meat or poultry, or to report food tampering, call the FDA during business hours at 1-888-674-6854 and after business hours at 1-800-233-3935.

868. Tip—Corn starch and arrow root may be substituted for flour as a thickener. Remember to use half the amount of corn starch or arrow root as you would flour.

869. Tip—Always mix corn starch and arrow root in cold water before adding to any hot ingredients.

870. Tip—To keep raisins and cranberries from sinking in batter, coat the raisins with flour before mixing into batter.

871. Tip—When making custards, remember to drizzle the cold mixture into the hot mixture as you are whisking and you won't need to strain the custard before baking.

872. Tip—Don't want to pay the price for expensive saffron? Don't! Try substituting turmeric.

873. Tip—Save your butter wrappers in a bag in the freezer and use them to grease baking pans.

874. Tip—When measuring honey or molasses, measure oil first so that sticky ingredients will slip out of the measuring cup.

875. Fact—Gelatin made with fresh pineapple or kiwi will not set.

876. Tip—Internal Temperatures for Cooked Meat:

Beef, lamb, and veal (steaks and roasts)	145°F for medium rare 160°F for medium
Ground meats (beef, pork, veal, and lamb), pork (chops, ribs, and roasts), and egg dishes	160°F
Ground turkey and chicken, stuffing, casseroles, and leftovers	165°F
Chicken and turkey (breasts)	170°F
Chicken and turkey (whole bird, legs, thighs, and wings)	180°F

877. Tip—USDA FSIS: http://www.fsis.usda.gov/oa/topics/foodsec _cons.pdf.

878. Tip—Can't remember which eggs are hard-boiled? Spin the egg, and if it wobbles, it is hard-boiled.

879. Tip—I use a pencil and write a large capital 'H' on hard-boiled eggs. Don't use ink or markers, as they bleed through the shells.

880. Tip—To keep boiled eggs from getting a gray ring around the yolk, remember to plunge them in ice water immediately after cooking.

881. Tip—Use clothes pins for potato chip bag clips. They are a lot less expensive than bag clips and for some reason they don't disappear.

882. Tip—Honey that becomes grainy can be heated and restored to a smooth texture.

883. **Tip**—When picnicking, layer ice with rock salt in a cooler to keep soda cold longer.

884. **Tip**—Frozen peas and corn can be used for ice packs. I write "ice pack" on the plastic bag with a permanent marker so that it will not become mixed up with frozen vegetables to be eaten.

885. **Tip**—To make sour milk, add 1 tablespoon of vinegar to 1 cup of milk and let stand for a couple of minutes.

886. **Tip**—Buttermilk can be substituted for any recipe that calls for sour milk.

887. **Tip**—Keep salt dry by placing a few grains of rice in the shaker.

888. **Tip**—After rolling out dough for dinner rolls, use a pizza cutter instead of a knife.

889. **Tip**—To prevent pizza crust from sticking to the baking stone, lightly sprinkle the stone with corn meal and then lay down the pizza crust dough.

890. **Tip**—To make self-rising flour, combine 1 cup of flour with 1 tablespoon of baking powder **or** 1 cup of flour with 1 teaspoon baking soda, 2 teaspoons cream of tartar, and ½ teaspoon salt. (I personally favor the second recipe.)

891. **Tip**—2 cups of sugar equals 1 pound.

892. **Tip**—2⅔ cup brown sugar equals a pound.

893. **Tip**—1 cup butter equals ½ pound.

894. **Tip**—1 ounce butter equals 2 tablespoons.

895. **Tip**—1 ounce of chocolate equals 1 square.

896. **Tip**—½ pound of nuts equals 1 cup.

897. **Tip**—1 square of chocolate equals 4 tablespoons of cocoa.

898. **Tip**—1 pound of apples, or 3 cups, is about 3 large apples.

899. **Tip**—1 pound of bananas is about 3 bananas.

900. **Tip**—1 pound of cottage cheese is about 2 cups.

901. **Tip**—One large marshmallow equals 10 small ones.

902. **Tip**—To brown meat in the skillet, pat dry with a paper towel.

903. Tip—For juicier meat, allow it to rest for 15 minutes before slicing.

904. Tip—Buy apples by the bushel and store in a cool dry place on wooden slats. Never place food containers directly on the cement. If time passes and apples start to wither, make applesauce or fruit leather. Don't forget to ask for a discount when buying large quantities.

905. Tip—Never store apples with cabbage, carrots, potatoes, or turnips unless you want your apples to taste like these vegetables.

906. Tip—To increase shelf life, winter squash needs to be cured for two weeks after picking. Curing squash is simple: store it in a warm, dry place for a couple of weeks. I typically pick my squash and just leave it in the garden for two weeks.

907. Tip—When winter squash is on sale, buy several and store them in a cool, dry place on wooden slats. My squash typically lasts 5 months. When the squash's shell starts to slightly soften, bake in the oven and freeze in freezer bags. By following these simple tips we have squash from our garden year round.

908. Tip—Root vegetables such as beets, potatoes, carrots, and turnips store well in a root cellar.

909. Tip—Onions and garlic need to be cured in temperatures around 80 degrees. Hang onions and garlic upside down by their stems where it is dry and there is good air circulation.

910. Tip—Onions and garlic need good air circulation, so store them in mesh bags or used panty hose hung from the rafters.

911. Tip—Save your dry slices of bread and make homemade bread crumbs. Break bread into small pieces and allow to dry on a cookie sheet. I drape a flour sack dish towel over the bread to protect from dust. Once dry, place in a food processor and pulse until they are to your liking and then store in a mason jar or plastic bag. If you are freezing then remember to fill the container to the very top so that it doesn't pick up any freezer taste.

912. Tip—If I am out of bread crumbs, I place croutons in my food processor to use as a substitute.

913. Fact—I once dropped my cell phone in the toilet. I remembered the salt and rice tip so I thought I would try using rice to dry out my cell phone. I hurried to the kitchen and covered my phone with rice and left it overnight. The next day my cell phone worked perfectly.

914. Tip—If you need a funnel and can't find one, just cut the top of a plastic soda bottle off and pour away!

915. Tip—If you need to cool cookies and you have run out of cooling racks, just place them on brown paper grocery bags.

916. Tip—To remove insects from vegetables, use 1 cup of salt per sink full of water and soak. The insects will float to the top.

917. Tip—I use unflavored dental floss to smoothly cut cheesecake.

918. Tip—Adding a pan of hot water to the oven while baking cheesecakes reduces cracking.

919. Tip—To get a crusty finish on French bread, place an empty pie pan on the lower shelf in a cold oven. Preheat oven and place loaves on baking rack per recipe. Once loaves are in oven, pour 1 cup of boiling water into the pie pan and quickly close the oven door.

920. Tip—Heat your ice cream scoop in hot water to make scooping less of a chore.

921. Tip—Heat a knife in warm water before cutting through a frosted cake and the frosting is less likely to stick to the knife.

922. Tip—Make an inexpensive and handy fruit and vegetable wash by mixing equal parts of vinegar and water.

923. Tip—To prevent cookies or brownies from drying out, I add a slice of bread to the container. This is especially helpful when sending care packages off to children!

924. Tip—To keep brown sugar from going hard, place a piece of waxed paper on top of the brown sugar followed by a slice of bread.

925. Tip—Hard brown sugar can be microwaved for a minute or so, and it will soften.

926. Tip—To reduce the fat of baked goods, substitute ½ of the oil called for with applesauce.

927. Tip—If you are out of brown sugar and can't run to the grocery store, remember this handy substitution: 1 cup white sugar plus 4 tablespoons molasses. I mix the molasses in with my liquids and the white sugar in with the dry ingredients.

928. Tip—A good rule of thumb for replacing honey for sugar in baked goods is an even exchange up to 1 cup; for every 1 cup of honey, decrease the amount of liquids by ¼ cup, add ½ teaspoon baking soda to the recipe, and decrease the baking temperature by 25°F. (I personally like substituting only half of the sugar with honey because honey is a great deal sweeter than sugar and has a stronger flavor.)

929. Fact—The US Food and Drug Administration, the Centers for Disease Control and Prevention, and the American Academy of Pediatrics recommend that honey not be given to children under 1 year of age to avoid risk of botulism.

930. Tip—If your cake cracks when taking it out of a pan, make cake bites instead.

931. Tip—Rather than using cheesecloth for my herbs and spice bouquets, I put them in a tea ball and cook as I normally would.

932. Tip—When I need ultrafine sugar, I place regular white granulated sugar in my food processor and blend it until it is "ultrafine." Be sure to process small amounts for best results.

933. Tip—I make my lasagna without cooking the noodles. The night before, I layer my lasagna ingredients as I normally would. By the next day the noodles are as soft as if they had been boiled before layering. Bake as you normally would.

934. Tip—½ teaspoon cream of tartar and ¼ teaspoon baking soda can be substituted for 1 teaspoon baking powder.

935. Tip—If you are out of heavy cream and need 1 cup, you may substitute ⅓ cup butter and ¾ cup milk.

936. Tip—Heavy cream and whipped cream are not the same. If a recipe calls for one cup *heavy cream,* it means cream poured straight from the carton. If it calls for 1 cup *whipped cream,* it means that the cream needs to be whipped, then measured.

937. Tip—If a recipe calls for *1 cup almonds, chopped,* it means to measure out 1 cup of almonds and then chop. If the recipe calls for *1 cup chopped almonds* it means chop almonds until you have a cup's worth.

938. Fact—Yogurt becomes runny if you stir it vigorously. So if you are incorporating other ingredients into it, be gentle with the yogurt by folding the ingredients in, not mixing.

939. Tip—Substitute yogurt for buttermilk by mixing equal portions of yogurt and water.

940. Tip—Yogurt can be substituted for sour cream in baked goods.

---

941. Recipe—Yogurt Pancakes

1½ cup flour

1 cup milk

¼ cup sugar

1 egg

¾ tsp. baking soda

¼ tsp. baking powder

¼ cup oil

1 cup yogurt

Mix all ingredients except yogurt. Then fold in yogurt. Ladle pancake batter onto a hot, oiled griddle. Flip when pancakes bubble and edges are brown.

Saving on Water, Electricity, Heat, and Other Household Expenses

942. **Tip**—Check to see if you have a leak in your toilet tank by placing food coloring in the tank. If the bowl water colors, then you have a leak. Fixing that leak will save you gallons of water per year.

943. **Tip**—Fix dripping faucets. If it will be a while before you can fix the leak, place a bowl under the dripping faucet and use the captured water for plants, garden, or lawn.

944. **Fact**—One drop per second from a leaking faucet adds up to 2,700 gallons of water per year.

945. **Tip**—If you do not have secondary water, catch rainwater from your house gutters for your garden.

946. **Tip**—To save water, *don't* leave water running while brushing your teeth or shaving! Yes; this is a pet peeve of mine!

947. **Tip**—Use old pet drinking water to water plants.

948. **Tip**—Let the dishes in the dishwasher drip dry instead of using the heated dry cycle. In the evening after the dishes have been washed, prop the door open and by morning most of them will be dry.

949. **Tip**—Modern dishwashers are powerful enough to wash dishes without requiring prewashing. In fact, most dishes just need to be scraped clean of large particles of food to come out clean.

950. **Tip**—Don't run tap water to heat it. Fill the cup and microwave it.

951. **Tip**—If you have to run the tap water, catch the water in a pan and water your pets, flowers, garden, or even houseplants.

952. **Tip**—If you drink only half of your glass of water at dinner, don't pour it down the sink, water your plants or fill the pet water dish.

953. **Tip**—Plan run-through-the-sprinkler days for your children on the days you are already planning on watering the lawn.

954. **Tip**—Wash cars and trucks at car washes; you will work more quickly when you are trying to beat the time, thereby using less water than doing it at home.

955. Tip—If you wash your cars and trucks at home, attach a sprayer to the hose so that you can conveniently turn the water on and off between scrubbing and rinsing.

956. Tip—Save water by sweeping sidewalks and driveways rather than spraying with the hose.

957. Tip—During the day when no one is home, lower your heat in the winter (or turn the AC down in summer).

958. Tip—Keep drapes closed during the heat of the day in the summer and open them in the winter. It's amazing how much heat is generated by sunlight coming through windows.

959. Tip—Turn off lights when not in the rooms.

960. Tip—Don't turn lights on during the day; more often than not, lights are turned on out of habit rather than need during daylight hours. For instance, I turn on the bathroom light only in the morning while putting on my makeup; during my shower and while dressing, the light from the bathroom window is sufficient.

961. Tip—Don't dress like it is summer in the winter! Wear sweaters in the house and save money. I lowered our temperature and we saved over $35.00 a month on utilities.

962. Tip—Once my children were old enough, I began leaving the oven door open after I baked to heat the house in the winter.

963. Tip—Using a slow-cooker instead of the oven during the summer will help keep your house cooler.

964. Tip—Bake multiple items to save energy. Rather than bake one loaf of bread, bake four loaves and freeze the other three. Bake your rolls or desserts for the week. It saves time and energy! After baking, I allow the oven to cool, and when it's warm, I ripen my yogurt in it.

965. Tip—Save energy by cooking with lids on pots and frying pans.

966. Tip—Keep closets and spare bedroom doors closed when not in use. I also close the registers and vents in spare rooms to reduce heating and cooling bills in the winter.

967. Tip—In the summer, I do my baking in the early morning and open the windows so that I don't heat up my house.

968. Tip—We grill a lot in the summer to keep the house cool and because I love grilled foods, especially grilled vegetables.

969. Tip—Lower the furnace temperature once everyone is in bed sleeping under a pile of blankets. I sleep better if the room is cold and I am snuggled down under a few quilts, and you may too.

970. Tip—Change your air conditioner and furnace filters monthly.

971. Tip—Shade your air conditioner unit; it will cool more efficiently.

972. Tip—Trim and protect your air conditioner from grass and weeds so that they won't get into the baffling.

973. Tip—In the fall, cover your air conditioner so that it doesn't get debris in it.

974. Tip—Change the direction of ceiling fans according to the seasons; counterclockwise in winter to push the rising warm air down to the floor, and during the summer, clockwise to pull the warm air up.

975. Tip—If your dryer has a moisture sensor, use it rather than a timed dry. It is better for your clothes and saves electricity.

976. Tip—Clean the lint catcher in your dryer before every load. This increases air flow and decreases the length of time you need to run your dryer, resulting in energy savings.

977. Tip—Use warm water with cold water rinses for washing clothes.

978. Tip—Don't use more clothes washing detergent than called for. This practice saves your pocketbook and also keeps your clothes from becoming dingy from detergent residue.

979. Tip—Only wash full loads of laundry.

980. Tip—Applying mulch to plants saves water.

981. Tip—Lower your hot water heater to 120°F. This will reduce your utility bill, decrease mineral build up, and more importantly, prevent scalding of skin.

982. Fact—According to *USA Today*, about 112,000 people each year are scalded from hot water and admitted to hospitals. They further state that 80percent of those admitted to the hospital are young children, the elderly, and the physically impaired.

983. Tip—If you are burned by heat, make sure to hold the area under cold water for 3 minutes. **Do not** apply butter, ice, lotion, or ointment to the burn. If my gram were alive, she would be feeling guilty because I once burned myself at her home and she rubbed butter on the flaming hot blister. Yes, she fried my skin even more—but hey, it was done with love.

984. Tip—While on vacation, lower the heat setting on your hot water heater. Why pay for hot water when no one will be using it?

985. Tip—Use less water by taking showers instead of baths. Well, that is, unless you have teenagers. My teenagers would take 30 minute showers; I finally had to set a kitchen timer in the bathroom, and when they had used their 10 minutes, I threatened to turn off the hot water to the house.

986. Tip—Install low-flow showerheads.

987. Tip—When watering our garden, I hand water each plant rather than irrigate or use sprinklers; not only do I save water, but I also have the opportunity to inspect my plants for insects and pull a few weeds while I am at it.

988. Tip—Keeping your grass a little taller in the summer cuts down on the amount of watering needed by shading the roots from the drying sun.

989. Tip—Save water by watering your grass instead of the sidewalk. Periodically check if sprinklers are watering what they are supposed to be watering.

990. Tip—To use even less water while showering, wet your body, turn off the water, lather up, then rinse.

991. Tip—Create a low-flow toilet by placing a water-filled plastic container in the tank. Saving water is great, but don't overdo it by placing too many plastic jugs in your tank or the toilet will not flush properly.

992. Tip—**Never** use bricks to create a low-flow toilet because they disintegrate and can clog your toilet.

993. Tip—To save water in the summer, wash your pets on the grass rather than in the bathtub. Your pets get a bath, and your grass gets watered.

994. Fact—Electronic devices use electricity even when not turned on. Plug electronic devices into a power strip and turn off the strip when not in use.

995. Tip—For more energy-saving ideas, check out the US Department of Energy website: http://www.energysavers.gov.

996. Fact—When I was a child, my mother would tape heavy plastic over the windows in the old home we rented to cut down on cold air leaking in from the windows. It really made a difference in the heating bill.

997. Tip—Check your cell phone for extra charges. I discovered that I was being charged for fees that I didn't agree to and were not part of my contract.

998. Tip—Every two years, when my cell phone contract is up, I check with competitors to see if I can get a better deal. The last time I did this, I managed to trim my monthly phone bill by $30.00, increase our minutes by 200, add unlimited texting, add another child to our plan, and get three free phones.

999. Tip—Cut back on cable services that you aren't using or that you rarely use. A case in point is a friend who pays $69.99 a month for basic cable. They watch a few documentaries a month but nothing else. They also go to the movies a few times a month. This seemed like a waste of money to me, so I suggested that they cancel their cable services and instead pay for home-delivered DVDs for a flat monthly fee of $10.00 a month.

1000. Tip—Check to see if creditors offer discounts for bills paid in full before the due date. I learned about this while building our house. It saved us 5–6 percent off of many building supply and labor bills.

1001. Tip—If you have an extra room, consider renting it out.

1002. Tip—When I go on girl shopping trips, I only take the amount of money I have budgeted to spend and leave my credit and debit cards at home; this way I never go over my budget with impulse buying.

The Virtues of a Provident Woman

By Trent Snow

A provident woman understands that "a penny saved is two pennies earned." She is a wise steward of her family's resources; she understands finance, keeps to her budget, and avoids the trappings of debit. In actuality, a provident woman can stretch a dime into a quarter even in today's economy.

A provident woman is not a compulsive shopper. She is a patient shopper. She is a wise shopper. She is a thrifty shopper. A provident woman knows a good deal when she sees one. She carefully conducts consumer research before purchasing, comparing and examining all aspects of a purchase, and finally determining what the best value for her family's needs is. She does not compromise quality for price; she understands and utilizes market strategies, sale cycles, promotional seasons, discounts, coupons, and volume discounts to her advantage.

A provident woman provides a buffer for her family against the storms of life. She provides a sense of security to her family through carefully planning for a rainy day—a day when there might be a lay-off, sickness, death, or disaster. She does this through prayerful and thoughtful planning, recycling, and managing her family's income; having a little savings tucked away; and storing food, water, and supplies in the pantry and closet for when the storms of life descend.

A provident woman understands the importance of inexpensive wholesome recreation, family vacations, Christmases, and other special occasions. She understands that memories, laughs, and lots of love are the key ingredients for a great family outing. Because of her belief in fiscal responsibility, she will search for good deals, purchase in advance, and budget monthly for that long-awaited holiday or vacation. Why does a provident woman painstakingly research, plan, and save? Because she does not want her family to experience the stress of mounting credit card debt—it simply is not worth it when her husband is stressed, ornery, and preoccupied during the family vacation wondering how he is going to pay for all the "fun."

A provident woman takes time to learn healthful nutrition; basic first aid; and how to mend, sew, garden, cook, and preserve foods so that she can provide healthy nutrition and food security for those she loves. A provident woman understands that her knowledge is valuable and must be shared with others, most importantly the next generation so that they will be independent, healthy, financially secure, and empowered.

A provident woman makes a house a home with her cheerful disposition, gentle touch, timely sense of humor, and never-ceasing compassion. A provident woman takes care of her family, her community, and herself spiritually, temporally, and emotionally. Charity and a love for all is her example.

A provident woman's family rests in comfort knowing that she is a wise and thoughtful steward of her family and their resources. Her family's trust in her is not in vain because they know that through her provident living skills and the blessings of God, their needs will be met even in trying times.

You may think that a provident woman does not exist. This is not true because I know such a woman, and her name is Michelle and I happen to be married to her. I love this provident woman deeply and thank the Lord daily for having Michelle in my life.

"Queen of Common Cents" is a collection of some of the practices that Michelle uses in our home. I hope that your family will be blessed as much as our family has been by these simple and prudent tips.

About the Author

Michelle is a graduate of Arizona State University, Utah State University, and the University of Utah. She sometimes is a little picked on at home by the BYU Cougars in her life: husband Trent, daughter Rachel, and son Tyler. Fortunately for Michelle, her other three children, Austen, Bryson, and Adam are remaining neutral at this point in time.

Please visit Michelle's website: www.michelle-snow.com,
And her blog: www.queenofcommoncents.blogspot.com.